DONS AND STUDENTS

BRITISH UNIVERSITIES TODAY

by John H. MacCallum Scott

The Plume Press Limited
IN ASSOCIATION WITH Ward Lock Limited
116 Baker Street, London W1

First published in 1973
by The Plume Press Limited
in association with Ward Lock Limited
116 Baker Street, London WIM 2BB
Copyright © John H. MacCallum Scott 1973

ISBN 0 7063 1491 3 hardback
       0 7063 1492 1 paperback

Printed in Great Britain
by Richard Clay (The Chaucer Press) Ltd
Bungay, Suffolk

This portrai... must be returned immed-
to illumina... ... or by the Librarian,
reader and, more especiall... ... st ... te.

The author traces the modern university's heredity
from Athens and mediaeval Europe to Britain's
civic universities of the nineteenth century and then
to the 'plate-glass' universities of the last decade. He
examines university organisation and the changes that
have taken place in the attitudes of both dons and
students and also the relationships that exist between
both don and don, and don and student. He concludes
by making some valuable suggestions about the shape
of universities and their possible future.

Contents

Preface

For some fifteen years of my life, between 1957 and 1972, I have been increasingly interested in our universities, first as a publisher of academic books, and later—since 1969—as Secretary to the Independent University Planning Board. Over these years I gradually grew into a devoted don-watcher, an occupation as fascinating as bird-watching and intellectually more intriguing.

This book is one of the products of these years. It should not be considered a deeply researched study of our universities. It is the product of observation and discussion. Unlike the bird-watcher, the don-watcher can talk with the objects of his interest and share with them their hopes and fears, thoughts and ambitions. Like bird-watching, on the other hand, he is concerned with a group or class of being of whom comparitively little is generally known. The academic world has until recently stood apart from the mainstream of life and is still something of a mystery to the general public. Other professions impinge on our daily lives to a degree that the academic profession does not. Only graduates have had experience of it and they still amount to only a small percentage of the population.

I became increasingly aware of the need for a book that would attempt to explain the academic world to a larger circle. That is my sole excuse for this volume.

All universities differ: there is not one that could be described as typical. To illustrate the general principles of university organisation and practice, therefore, I have been driven to invent a university of my own—the University of Bolderdale—which appears from time to time throughout the following pages. It is a purely imaginary institution which should in no way be taken as a portrait of any existing university. The dons and administrators with whom I have peopled it are equally imaginary, and as far as I am aware could not be identified with any individual academics working in universities today. The virtues and frailties depicted through this device are not, however, untypical. If I have any regret it is that I did not take to the academic life and become a don myself.

I should like to acknowledge a number of personal obligations to those who have helped me.

In the first place, I must thank the many hundreds of dons and students who spared time to talk with me in the course of my work as a publisher. They were no more aware than I was at the time that they were helping to create the infrastructure of this book, and I can only hope that none of them will now regret their kindness. I also thank Professor Max Beloff and Mr Ralph Harris for reading portions of the typescript and making valuable comments on them. Neither should be held in any way responsible for the book's final form. I thank Mr Frank Herrmann for the insistence without which I would never have embarked on it and for the persistance without which I would never have completed it.

My wife undertook the gargantuan task of transforming my illegible manuscript into a legible typescript, and also offered many forceful criticisms which were taken to heart. Miss Molly Clements and Mrs Colin Calvert very kindly retyped the final text, which of course I amended yet again, and left to Miss Candida Geddes to make fit for the printer.

CHAPTER ONE

Introduction

'The only use of Oxford is that it is a place for *study*, a refuge from the world and its claims,' said the Prince Consort when the education of His Royal Highness Prince Albert Edward was under discussion. It was a not uncommon opinion. As far as the public of that day was aware even of the existence of universities, they were looked on as remote monastic establishments, far from the world of affairs. This picture was a caricature, concentrating on a single view of its subject but ignoring its full variety. It was the world that stood apart from the universities, not the other way round.

Far from being remote, universities have always been acutely aware of the world beyond their own walls. It could hardly have been otherwise when the bulk of their membership were young men who had come out of that world for a sojourn of a few years, all of them reflecting it and most of them intending to return to it. The world may have paid very little attention to universities, but the study of man and his environment has always been, and remains, one of the prime purposes of every university worth the name. The legend of the ivory tower was never more than a popular myth, born out of ignorance. The learned and the learners were rarely appreciated by men of affairs until after the industrial revolution, when science and technology began to influence every aspect of daily life.

Ignorance about universities was widespread in the nineteenth century. Sir Sydney Caine has made the point that for the great novelists of that period they were virtually non-existent. Dickens does not have a single don in his gallery of characters. Nor, offhand, could I name one in Thackeray's works. In Trollope's novels they make fleeting, shadowy, appearances; Mr Arabin only acquired importance for the reader after he had left Oxford. Perhaps the most pungent comment on the standing of universities in the public mind is that the first really successful novel with a university background was Max Beerbohm's devastating cartoon of Oxford life at the turn of the century, *Zuleika Dobson*. Since then, writers of detective stories have found in the university a useful setting full of the eccentricities that make a good murder plot faintly plausible;

and the comic don eventually became good for a laugh in a straight novel or a light play. It was not until C. P. Snow began to write seriously about it that academic life in the raw held any interest for the general reader. Universities have been a long time in making their mark with the public.

One day, no doubt, the full story of how they came to do so will be written; but so far none of the dons who specialises in social historical research has tackled the subject. There seems to be a taboo on research into the researchers. I suppose it amounts to a kind of incest.

To the outsider, however, the subject can be a fascinating one. Comparing the ancient foundations—Oxford or St Andrews or Trinity, Dublin—with the Sussexes, Kents, Lancasters and Warwicks of the 1960s, there seems to have been almost an evolutionary leap. The missing link is, of course, to be found in the great civic universities founded in the nineteenth century—London, Manchester, Bristol, Liverpool and their like. Perhaps the future is foreshadowed by the Open University, chartered at the end of the 1960s, but that is improbable. It certainly has a function to perform, but as an alternative, not as a substitute.

An immediate result of the sudden impact of universities on the public consciousness has been the growth of many misconceptions about their nature and purpose. A secondary result, particularly since they are now almost completely supported out of public funds, has been an increasing tendency to teach the universities their business, to look on them as part of the state machine. This combination of confusion and control presents a serious threat to their future, and one of the purposes of this book is to try to present a rounded portrait both of the universities as they are today and of the people who work in them. It is also, however, intended for the student. His years at university are likely to be the most significant in his life, setting much of the tone for his future. It is not just a matter of taking a degree. A university has a great deal more to offer than instruction in this or that field of knowledge. It is, or should be, a close-knit community in which each group—undergraduates, graduates, teachers, researchers and administrators—is linked with all the others, and those who identify themselves most closely with its totality get the most out of it. The university, covering the whole known range of human knowledge, offers breadth of interest and a training of the mind far beyond the limits of any one discipline, but like any other institution its best prizes go to those who understand it well enough to make the most of it. Not enough is done today to prepare the student for university life.

The university is, moreover, a key factor in the process of civilisation, providing the continuity and expansion of knowledge by which each generation climbs up on the shoulders of the last. Before the West fought its way out of the Dark Ages, it established universities. At first they taught the basic subjects of medicine, law and theology, the three fundamental sciences of man, society and God. Later, as their probing into reality developed, they added new subjects such as grammar, rhetoric and dialectic, mathematics, music, geometry and astronomy. That was in mediaeval times, when centres of learning were few in number and only loosely organised, still struggling to bring some order into the assault on ignorance. The attack on one subject opened up new fields of speculation. The unity of all knowledge was the first great university discovery.

Like the America of the eighteenth and early nineteenth centuries, the academic world faces the challenge of a frontier. The American frontier was limited by the further ocean (at any rate until Neil Armstrong set foot on the moon), but the frontier of knowledge is like the Hydra: every new advance opens up new avenues of research. Universities are not the only institutions that carry out this probe into reality. There are, for instance, learned institutes, free from the burden of teaching, that specialise in detailed research into their own subjects, but they make no provision for their own futures. Without universities to feed them with trained and able recruits they would wither and die. Dons are different from lawyers, doctors, accountants, engineers, churchmen. They share something with all those professional groups, but what is uniquely theirs, and what they all recognise as uniquely theirs, is their position at the frontier. It was the academic community that was at root responsible for the conquest of space, that stimulated the first heart transplant, that developed the concept of democratic government, that created the science of economics and set the stage for the production of the atom bomb. It was Hitler's repression of his academics that lost him a war.

The university is both a teaching establishment and a research insti-tute. Its purpose is to transmit existing knowledge, imperfect as it must be, to the next generation, and to train its students in the art and tech-niques of inquiry into the unknown. Because of this double function, every competent don is in some degree a schizophrenic. He knows that what he teaches is only an approximation to truth, and is continually goaded into questioning his command of his own subject. He is always under the temptation to turn aside from the task of transmitting error to the frustrating, but occasionally wildly rewarding ability to cry at last, 'Eureka'. The best teacher is often the best researcher, provided he is so built as to be able to give equal effort to both functions. He is able to teach not only what he knows, but also what he does not know. He can bring his students right up to the frontier as well as help them to think about what lies on its conquered side. Yet the temptation to go off on a lonely safari must be strong, which is why the university is constantly in danger of temporarily losing touch, not with its pursuit of ultimate reality, but with the reality of the world it exists to serve. Even if it does lose touch with that world it still serves a useful purpose, but it is different in quality. The process I described as an apparent 'evolutionary leap' was in fact a slow transfer from the university of the mind to the university of involvement in practical affairs.

The modern British university is being brought more and more closely into direct association with the everyday world—too closely for its own good, some might say; not closely enough, say some of the zealots for change. Since the second world war the academic community has been under two complementary sets of pressures. On the one hand, it is being forced to expand at a rate far beyond its power of assimilation; on the other, it is faced by the challenge of the technological revolution in all its facets. As we shall see in the next chapter, the number of university students has doubled in the last two decades, and current planning is based on an even greater expansion in the future. This has involved not only a change in the balance of student types, but also a serious dilution of academic staff, not unlike the swamping of trained cadres at an outbreak of war; while the financial problems it has brought in its train have led to an increasing degree of political control in a field of endeavour where independence has always been a prized and essential asset. It is not surprising that disquiet among staff and discontent among students should be the two most significant features of university life today. Many dons of the old school find it difficult to sympathise with the motivations of the modern student, and many of the younger dons lack adequate understanding of the traditions of academic purpose. Similarly, large numbers of the new-type students see in the university only an extension of their schooling and look to it for no more than a qualification that will be useful in their careers. Naturally, they tend to be impatient of what seem to them to be the irrelevancies of the academic approach.

Side by side with the problems presented by over-rapid expansion, the universities find themselves in a world where sudden technological advance has produced changes so far-reaching as to amount almost to a change in quality. Science itself has entered on so many new avenues of study, ranging from the inner recesses of micro-biology to the further limits of the outer nebulae, that it is impossible for any one university to comprehend them all, and individual institutions find themselves under the need to devote a growing proportion of their resources to the scientific and technical disciplines. The threat to the humanities is still latent, but the pressure to relegate them to second place grows stronger every year, particularly since it has the backing of the state with its control of the purse strings. These recent developments have not helped to ease the tensions that form an inevitable part of community life. It is only quite recently that academics have begun to speak openly of the 'two cultures', a concept foreshadowed over half a century ago by H. G. Wells and developed by C. P. Snow. They have been driven to it by the exaggeration of the ancient philosophical dilemma posed by the differences between empiricist and rationalist. Is experiment or thought the true source of progress? The scientists would say experiment; many philosophers and most theologians would say thought. Although it is the age-old dispute between materialist and idealist, it has been given a new twist by the enormous strides the materialists have taken over the last fifty years and especially over the last twenty. Universities have come to be divided between the two, with the scientists running well ahead. Now, humane studies have begun to fight back.

These tensions are a direct result of the scientific and technological explosion of the last quarter-century. A secondary result has grown out of the new ease of communication that technology has made possible. There are two aspects of communication in this context, speed and mass. The limitations to both have virtually been annihilated. Distance has lost importance and, as Marshall McLuhan has pointed out, reproduction is now no longer confined to the output of a printing press. The annihilation of distance, though politicians can still contrive to erect new barriers, has brought the academic communities of all countries into much closer and more immediate contact than had been possible in earlier days. Dons have become world travellers, and the ancient tradition of the wandering scholar is being revived on a new and massive scale. This is what the authors of *1066 and All That* would have called a 'Good Thing'. The development of radio and television has provided vast new audiences and offers entirely new methods of transmitting knowledge. The universities are faced with the need to revise their whole approach to teaching.

A third impact on learning comes from the computer. Although computer science is barely twenty-five years old, it seems to have penetrated virtually every academic discipline by presenting the researcher with a new tool of unforeseen power. It can store, clarify and relate information to a degree that would have been unthinkable twenty years ago. But the computer, for all its ability to define the authorship of St Paul's Epistles or to illuminate the voting behaviour of Little Stokum-in-Mud, is primarily a mathematical instrument, and its arrival has boosted mathematics to a senior place in most universities by imposing on students in nearly every field a need for some mathematical knowledge.

The pursuit of knowledge is very largely a matter of methodology, of the mechanism of inquiring and learning, and these new techniques have given immense impetus to the quantitative and analytical approach. The statistician is being elevated to the level of the Witch of Endor. Numbers are being given more weight than reason, not because they are better but because they are easier to manipulate with the new mechanical aids. The academic community is in danger of becoming softwear. This would be a Bad Thing.

Weakened by dilution and battered by technology, the university world is going through a difficult period. The change is most immediately visible in the new architecture. The mellow, cloistered charm of the ancient foundations and the stately dignity of redbrick are giving way to the functional building with its calculated allotment of space, its science-fiction design, its managerial aura and the vision of 'broiler B.A.s' it automatically conjures up. At a deeper level, less obvious to the lay observer, disquiet is spreading among dons, together with a degree of dissatisfaction among students even more profound than their occasional spectaculars seem to indicate.

I have explained that this book is written, in some measure, for the student. It is also very largely *about* dons. All university history shows a constantly recurring thread of love–hate relationship between the two groups. The love has tended to be confined to relations between individuals, but the hate has been a group phenomenon, usually more active among the students. At the moment, the hate element is predominant, fanned by the difficulties I have touched on in the last paragraphs. Yet the interests of the two groups are identical. Both groups are learners, each in their own way and on their own level. The art of learning is their prime concern, and if dons also teach, it is because one of the products of their teaching is the next generation of learners who will take on where they leave off the expansion of the frontiers of knowledge. The relation between don and student is an organic one, almost a family relationship, embodying all the tensions of family life. In this sense the don finds himself to some degree *in loco parentis* and his success or failure depends on the wisdom and tolerance he can bring to his task. In the same way, the student finds himself *in statu pupillarii*, as it is still called in the ancient foundations, and owes a responsibility, not for submission which is not in the nature of the young, but for eagerness to make the most of what he is offered. The don's responsibility is not necessarily higher, but it is certainly more crucial. If this book was being written for dons, it would be mostly about students, but it is the other way round. All the same, I hope a lot of dons will read it too, if only for the therapy recommended by Burns: 'tae see oorsels as ithers see us'.

Before looking specifically at dons, however, we must first take a quick but comprehensive look at the academic world of today, both at home and in its global setting; then we must look back to its roots and see something of the tradition that has moulded it. To complete the prologue, we must look at current university organisation, at the nuts and bolts of the mechanism through which it achieves, or tries to achieve, its purpose. So long a preamble is a necessary background to a portrait of the dons themselves. It will be a 'warts and all' portrait, more inclined to criticism than to praise. Dons are apt to praise themselves sufficiently as it is. Finally, there will be some words about students and student/don relationships.

What I write will, I hope, be useful to students, particularly to freshmen who should be helped to understand more than they do of the new world into which they are moving. But I hope it will also help to interpret to a wider public the importance of the university to society and its key role in maintaining and strengthening the basis of our civilisation.

CHAPTER TWO

The British universities[1]

In the first decades of the nineteenth century there were two universities in England and four in Scotland. Oxford and Cambridge had grown slowly as centres of learning from early mediaeval days, but their formal foundation is usually reckoned as that of their first colleges—University College in the case of Oxford in 1249, and Peterhouse at Cambridge in 1284. In Scotland, St Andrews was founded in 1411, Glasgow in 1453, Aberdeen in 1494 and Edinburgh in 1582. A gap of over two centuries followed until the University of Durham was established in 1832.

By 1936, there were eleven universities in England, four in Scotland and four in Wales (though the Welsh universities were, and still are, officially grouped under a single University of Wales) and one in Northern Ireland. In the last thirty years the number has risen to thirty-four in England, eight in Scotland, five in Wales and two in Northern Ireland.

To complete the picture of the British Isles as a whole, one should include Trinity College, Dublin, which was founded in 1591 (and therefore ranks as one of the ancient foundations) and the National University of Ireland with its three colleges of Dublin, Cork and Galway. These, however, now stand outside the British university system, and are subject to the laws of the Irish Republic.

The universities founded in the nineteenth and early twentieth centuries were municipal in character, designed in the main to provide for their own neighbourhoods. (This was largely true also of the Scottish universities, though St Andrews always enjoyed an international reputation.) They were evidence of the growing demand for higher education stimulated by the Industrial Revolution and the rise of the middle classes. Though they tended to be more vocational in character than the ancient foundations and put a proportionately greater emphasis on science and technology, they did not neglect the humanities and before long their degrees had won respect not only at home but throughout the Empire. They provided much talent for the universities of the new

[1] A table listing the British universities and the dates of their foundations will be found in the Appendix on page 149.

world. The soubriquet 'redbrick' derives more from social than from academic (or architectural, for that matter) reasons. Oxford and Cambridge remained the fashionable universities and, it must be admitted, continued to scrape most of the cream off the academic community, but with the increase in the numbers of Chairs and lectureships, and the competition this increase provoked, the academic community itself was becoming far larger, even in its higher quality, than the ancient foundations could themselves accommodate.

In spite of the fourfold increase in the number of foundations, from six to twenty-three (including Ireland) in just over a century, the academic community of the early 1900s still remained numerically a tiny proportion of the whole nation, and its impact on the generality of the people was negligible. They were as much aware of it as Kipps was aware of his 'choobs'.[1] It was not until the brave new world had been ushered in after 1945 that the academic community began to impinge seriously on the popular consciousness. In the euphoria of what was called victory nothing seemed out of reach of anyone and what had hitherto been the preserve of the few became the goal of the many. This was another Good Thing; nothing should be out of reach of the many although, as the late Lord Beveridge once reminded us, not everyone can be Archbishop of Canterbury just because he wants to. It became government policy to encourage the expansion of the universities to accommodate a greatly increased student body. By the academic year 1953–54 it had grown to almost 100,000 from 63,420 in 1938–39; by 1966–67 it was over 200,000. In the same thirteen years the academic staff had grown from 10,744 to 28,015. The academic community had at last become a sizeable slice of the population.

The increase has not been due entirely to the twenty-eight new universities established since the war. All the older institutions have mushroomed as well. The building programme has been prodigious. When I was touring the universities between 1967 and 1969 I never had any trouble finding them; all one had to look for was a forest of building cranes. Though the new universities have been dubbed 'plate-glass' to distinguish them from the older, and more sedate, redbrick of the nineteenth century, they have no monopoly of that material; Oxford's new St Catherine's College seems to display more of it than the whole of Sussex. In universities like Newcastle, Birmingham and Manchester, to name but a few, their original redbrick cores stand in rather dignified and stately contrast to the sometimes astonishing experiments of *avant-garde* architects that surround them. Stone, brick or concrete and glass,

---

[1] H. G. Wells's novel *Kipps* should be compulsory reading for all social scientists and psychologists.

it is not the material that shapes the university, though it probably has a subliminal effect on its development. It is the people who live and work in it who give it character and who are, along with the University Grants Committee, responsible for its architectural impact.

It is not surprising that the nature of universities should have undergone a more far-reaching change in the last thirty years than in the whole of the previous two centuries. With a shift in their class basis, new motivations have come into play. Class is often treated as a pejorative concept, but a change in class structure is a fact, to be neither welcomed nor condemned but accepted and understood. *Pace* the activist social scientists, its operation cannot be controlled, only acknowledged and allowed for.

Before discussing the change in the universities, however, we must first look at what they have changed from. Oxford and Cambridge were, in the inter-war years, at the sunset of what might be called the *Zuleika Dobson* period. Heavily anchored in the past, they continued to enjoy the prestige of social worth and outstanding standards of scholarship; they were still the haunt of wealthy but not necessarily very talented young men who went there as a matter of course, and a more numerous group of serious students, mainly drawn from the middle classes. In one sense they could almost be described as finishing schools at which the children of an hereditary élite were groomed to take their place in a traditional world. Though their scholarship was still superb, much of it lagged behind the requirements of a world that was about to erupt into Hitlerism, atomic fission, jet engines and the computer. Cambridge was the closer to contemporary reality of the two, but it still followed the ancient pattern. It was in the women's colleges that the change was most clearly foreshadowed. They were the thin end of the wedge, the challenge to tradition, the cloud no larger than a man's hand. Learning had been a male occupation. Shakespeare and Tennyson had imagined women's universities rather as Wells had imagined a time machine and Jules Verne his Nautilus, but both they and their contemporaries saw *Love's Labour's Lost* and *The Princess* as essays in futurism rather than as prophecies. Cambridge was the first to break through the barrier. Girton was established in 1873 and Newnham in 1875. Somerville, the first Oxford women's college, was established in 1879. Women were not admitted as full members of Oxford University until 1920. Here Cambridge fell behind; women were first admitted to Cambridge degrees in 1923.

The admission of women on equal terms with men[1] was a turning

---

[1] Equal only academically at first. They were for many years subjected—not least by the heads of their own colleges—to social restraints that no male under-

point in the history of the ancient universities, but it had taken some fifty years to bring about. The breaking of the class barrier took even longer, in spite of the part played in it by the nineteenth-century foundations. In theory, anyone in any age could go to university. In practice, the privilege was limited to those who could find some way of maintaining themselves while they studied which, with wages at nine-teenth- and early twentieth-century level, effectively excluded all but a tiny minority. The ambitious and exceptionally able might find an outside source of support. Some bright young men were supported by patrons—the origin of the scholarship system; the Church did much to help forward the poverty-stricken scholar; and local charities were formed to help promising youths on their way, but by and large univer-sities were open only to the sons of gentlemen, scholars and rich bourgeois; the children of the working class were excluded. Ruskin College, established in Oxford in 1925 by the TUC, was an early attempt at a breakthrough but it has not yet become an official part of the university.

Between the wars the scholarship system remained chiefly at the service of the middle classes as far as Oxford and Cambridge were concerned, but in provincial universities it was increasingly used to help the occasional bright young candidate from the working class. Human nature being what it is, the term redbrick thus came to carry a double pejorative implication. In addition to suggesting some degree of academic inferiority, there were undertones of social inferiority as well, which not even strong local patriotism could altogether ignore. The sons and daughters of the well-to-do classes of the West Country, the Midlands and the North still tended to seek places at Oxford or Cambridge rather than at establishments nearer home. It was, nevertheless, during this inter-war period that redbrick established itself as a serious competitor to the older foundations, and began to bring the whole academic world into closer touch with the twentieth century. By 1945, the stage was set for the big transformation scene.

Before turning to the newcomers of the nineteenth and twentieth centuries, it would be as well to look at the four Scottish universities, which had already contrived a merger between mediaeval and Victorian types of institution. The Scottish approach to education differed in quality and in breadth from the English, not least because their respec-tive class systems had developed along different lines. Class has always

---

graduate would have endured. Only recently there were still iron bars guarding the ground floor windows in Lady Margaret Hall, and nobody who heard Miss Dilys Powell recall her memories of Somerville will forget the drama of her rustication.

been more fluid north of the border, and education recognised as the most effective ladder for scaling such barriers as there were. A desire amounting almost to a lust for education, and an admiration for learning as a desirable achievement, were characteristic of a very wide range of Scottish society. There was a real market for scholarship, not just among the well-to-do but in the tradesmen and small farmer classes as well. To get at least one son to university was a primary aim of many Scottish parents. The competition was keen and by no means all succeeded, but there was never any want of candidates.

St Andrews followed the ancient model, and to this day has more in common with Oxford and Cambridge than with its fellows in Scotland; but Glasgow, Aberdeen and Edinburgh were more akin to the civic universities of the nineteenth century. They were established in urban centres, and were intended primarily for the sons of the local citizenry. Students flocked to them from the surrounding countryside, but they remained, Glasgow especially, civic in purpose. They had had a very long life, however, in comparison with their English cousins, and before these were founded had established strong academic traditions and won world-wide recognition for their degrees. In some measure, they set a pattern of development for redbrick to follow, and although redbrick has caught them up and in some cases surpassed them, they were the pioneers of the new academic form that was to become dominant, in numbers if not in reputation, by the 1930s.

Looking at it with the hindsight of thirty years, it would be fair to say that by 1939 the redbrick universities were the real basis for future advance. They had developed their own establishments and traditions. They were more closely in touch with the real demands of society than the ancient foundations. They were providing for a demand from a completely new, and hitherto uncatered for, sector of the population—the sons and daughters of the lower middle class and, though to a much lesser degree, of the working class. In this, they were in fact following the Scottish example, but it is probable that where there was any conscious imitation they were following an American lead. Britain was slowly becoming acquainted with the American way of life. The film had become a powerful conductor of American mores; so had the mass-produced Press with its insatiable demand for articles on every subject under the sun. In America the idea of a 'college education' was unrelated to social status. True enough, there were certain universities, especially in the east, where those of wealthy parentage were most likely to be found, but a college education was regarded, not as a right, but as a proper object of desire irrespective of class or wealth, and American society was organised to make it available on the widest possible scale. In other words, the Americans accepted the Scottish belief in higher education, but were more efficient in giving effect to it. To be 'working my way through college' was highly meritorious, and many were the magazine subscriptions and vacuum cleaners sold on American doorsteps by young men who introduced themselves with that emotive phrase. Not only was the young Briton's ambition to go to a university stirred by the American example, but also the British social conscience. It was between the wars, during the grand age of the movie and the talkie, that Britain's modern university system received its first impetus.

There was, however, to be a profound difference between the British universities of the post-war period and their Scottish/American proto-types, a difference rooted in continental European practice. Before the twentieth century the Continent made little impression on the broad stream of popular British thought. The insular British have rarely looked on foreigners as suitable objects for imitation. Americans are merely devient Englishmen; the French, Germans, Italians belong to a lesser order of creation. The late nineteenth century, however, ushered in the spread of socialist ideas, which were essentially continental in origin. The American example stimulated our desire for equality, the continental our means of achieving it. From the West came the logical development of the free economy; from our continental neighbours the idea of the planned society, with equality imposed from above rather than permitted and encouraged to make its way from below. As far as the universities were concerned, continental influence opened up two new paths of development: acceptance of the idea of the state university, which was the continental norm, on the one hand; and on the other, acceptance of the aim of free university education, which was not then a general part of continental practice but was a direct corollary of the socialist ideal.

The post-war British university system is, then, a closely interwoven tapestry of four complementary influences, no one of which is dominant. First, the traditional British belief in the university as a completely independent corporation free from all outside influence, dedicated to teaching and research. Second, the contradictory continental belief that higher education is a responsibility of authority, be it Church or state. Third, the American belief that a university education should be avail-able to all who want it and can profit from it. Fourth, the socialist theory, that not only is it the duty of the state, and in the interest of the com-munity as a whole, to provide university education out of public funds, but also that it is immoral and entirely wrong for any university to be other than state-operated. It is an odd and haphazard mixture, but not at all untypical of the hugger-mugger way in which most British institutions have evolved. Any clear understanding of our post-war university system must be sought in this peculiar heredity.

Since 1945 the number of British universities has been increased to 49, excluding the three in Eire—well over double the pre-war number. Not all of them are entirely new. Eight are based on University Colleges founded in an earlier period, ten others on Colleges of Advanced Technology also founded earlier and one on the Royal College of Art, which was chartered in 1896 and raised to university status in 1967. Ten were completely new foundations, while the former University Colleges can also be treated as new foundations since their redbrick cores are so small as to be virtually insignificant in the welter of new buildings that are planned to surround them. None of them had had the opportunity to establish strong academic traditions of their own while they were linked to other institutions. The university scene can therefore be broken down into four main types: the ancient foundations, redbrick, former CATs and the new universities. And now, piling Pelion upon Ossa, we have the Open University.

It would be unprofitable, indeed impossible, to discriminate between these types in terms of quality. Each fulfils an academic role of its own. Oxford and Cambridge remain unique, partly because of their college systems, partly because they both have more to offer both to dons and to students in the way of atmosphere and background. Akin to them is St Andrews, but it was comparatively small, and is now being expanded to the point at which the new is taking over from the old. The other three ancient foundations in Scotland have, as we have seen, more in common with the great civic universities we have already discussed. London, however, deserves a special word to itself. By far the largest in student numbers (though small compared to those of some capital cities overseas) it enjoys unique facilities in its metropolitan surroundings, and is able to attract a unique body of both staff and post-graduate students. But what it gains on those swings it tends to lose on the roundabouts of dispersal and anonymity. Instead of being closely grouped, it is scattered as widely as Hampstead, Mile End, Kensington, even Egham; students and staff disappear into the great whirl of metropolitan life, and the idea of a community is about as easy to establish as team spirit in a rush-hour crowd. Academic quality is not affected, but the intangibles of campus life are hard to come by. It is different in, say, Manchester or Glasgow, where there is a clearly demarcated area within which most of the university is congregated.

The new universities founded since the war are different not only in architecture and location (only Dundee stands at a city centre), but in academic character as well. They are all, necessarily, experimental, each devised by a planning board with one eye on excellence and the other on distinctiveness. Each one tries to break new ground—in the courses it offers, in the research it undertakes, in its student/teacher relationships. Keele was the first, starting in the old-fashioned way as a university college attached to the University of Manchester. Then in the late 'fifties and early 'sixties they burst out like a sudden rash—Exeter, Sussex, York, Lancaster, Warwick, East Anglia, Essex, Kent, Stirling and Ulster, all established in the space of a single decade. The mere fact of so many new institutions springing up together introduced a competitive element into the academic world alien to its traditions. The new universities are all highly extrovert. Each aims not only at reputation, but at a higher reputation than its rivals. They compete for good students and for staff. It is a strange form of competition, because there is no market element in it; salaries and fees are the same for all. They cannot lure away distinguished academics by promises of higher pay or undercut each other by reducing fees. To the dons they must offer better amenities, better research facilities, better opportunities for experiment, a better academic atmosphere; to the students, more up-to-date courses, better recreation facilities, better student/teacher relations. On the face of it nothing could be more calculated to produce a high standard of excellence, but it does not always work out that way. The obvious pitfalls have not always been avoided. The desire for distinctiveness can, and does on occasions, lead to crankiness. There is a thin line between good student/teacher relations and a failure in discipline. Experiments in architecture do not always produce perfection. Academic experiments can lead to academic nonsense. When a pot boils, it is what is left in the pot that counts, not the steam.

Finally, there are the former CATS. There are ten of them, all established before the second war and none making any pretence to university status. Their object was to train technicians, to teach the science and skills of technology. When, in the 1960s, they were granted the rank of universities, it was largely with the political aim of spreading the prestige of a degree to a wider sector of the working class. To give an air of verisimilitude to their assumption of this new role, the government grant was accompanied by an instruction to include an element of non-technical education in the courses offered. Their success in achieving this broader syllabus varies widely. Strathclyde has quite a substantial arts/social science element, the City University a minimal one, Brunel none at all apart from a department of economics. It is noteworthy that they have a considerably higher drop-out rate than the traditional universities, due to students not returning for the second half of their 'sandwich' courses. It is too early yet to say how they will develop, but they seem to fulfil their non-technical role uneasily. They find it difficult to compete for good staff in these fields.

A word should be added here about the Open University, which received its Royal Charter in 1969 and enrolled its first students in 1971. This is one of the wilder socialist experiments in education and it will not be possible to begin to judge it until the late 1970s. The idea of using radio, television and correspondence courses to provide higher education for an indeterminate body of students who need have no initial qualifications is an interesting one, and much in tune with the times. On the face of it, its degrees are unlikely to have the same value as those of the traditional universities, and the absence of communal life outside the residential fortnight offered once a year will rob its students of one of the most valuable features of university experience. Nevertheless, it is an experiment worth trying out.

A brief catalogue of the new universities does not begin to describe the gulf that lies between the academic world of the inter-war years and that of today. Student body, staff and academic practice have all suffered a sea change.

It would be fair to call the student body of yesterday a narrow élite. Today it is a larger and more broadly based élite. On the campus of the 1970s you will find the children of the small-town draper, the postman, the smallholder, the fitter and the man who reads the gas meter. These are not unique examples, though their actual numbers are fewer than is often asserted. Working class students number less than a quarter of the total student body. Nevertheless, they are significant of the changed basis of admission, for they owe their places not to their origin but to their own quality. They bring with them a new outlook, a new factor in the complex of university life. They have won their position, not inherited it, and they are well aware of the fact. They are paid for out of public funds, and they feel they are there by right. They are not always willing to be *in statu pupillarii*. They demand value, and are prepared to fight for it. They present the staff with the entirely new problem of how to organise teaching without the support of the traditional sanctions. Motivation, too, has changed. The student no longer seeks a university education for its own sake. The great rise in the number of degree holders means that the degree has lost something of its mystique. It has become a valuable economic asset, in the sense that it affects earning capacity. The student looks on it as capital and on his time at the university as a kind of savings or investment. Much of the clamour for 'participation' springs from the belief that he has a personal stake in the running of the institution, that in return for his work, which is laying the foundations of what he hopes will be a successful career, he is entitled to a say in its management. We need not consider the validity of that attitude at this stage, but it is widespread and by no means confined to the militants. Large numbers of students feel it intensely. The university is no longer an ante-room to life; it is life itself. This feeling goes deeper than the political consciousness that has always stirred students to protest. It is as highly personal as the workman's concern over his conditions of work, or a parent's care for his children's schooling. Moreover, as the proportion of students from working class homes rises, it brings with it the ethos of trade unionism and a tendency among students to unionise themselves. Nothing shows the change in climate more clearly than the emergence of the National Union of Students. Its management may be non-representative, but that is a common union phenomenon. The substantial support it gets in practice from students up and down the country shows that it is an actual force, not a mere hypothesis. In the 1930s its existence in its present form would have been inconceivable.

Alongside the class change in the student mix there has also been a sex change. More than a third of today's students are women. The old monasticism which had left its mark right through the 1930s has been shattered for good and all. Oxford and Cambridge have been least affected, but their defences have been breached; some colleges have already admitted women students and even All Souls has occasional ladies' nights in Hall. Sex has come to the universities with a vengeance, and is making up for lost time. Contraceptive advice, euphemistically and inaccurately described as family planning, is available on almost every campus. Engagements are common, and marriages increasing. As far as I know, the first university crèche has yet to be established, but it cannot be far off. This too is probably an advance, though less obviously so than the breakdown of the class barrier. It has at any rate dealt a mortal blow to the university red light districts of the past.

The changes in academic practice are less clear-cut. The academic mills grind slowly even though technology is forcing the pace. In every age the universities have had their special clients: to begin with the ancient professions of Church, medicine and law, to which were later added education and the first burgeoning of natural science. In the nineteenth century great demands were made by the developing art of government. It was to the universities that the state turned for its civil service both at home and overseas.

The British Empire was largely supported on an infrastructure of Greats and Modern Greats. Today's chief client is industry in all its ramifications, and universities are struggling to adjust their practice to its particular demands without abandoning their traditional purpose. The requirement is not altogether dissimilar from the earlier demand of government; the great industrial complexes have the same need for administrators and proconsuls who have studied the traditional disciplines in depth. A double First still opens the doors. But science and technology and economics are the key subjects, especially applied science and applied economics. Running them a close second is the exporter's need for staff with a wider knowledge of other countries. Centres of what are called area studies are springing up everywhere; modern languages have acquired a practical as well as a cultural value; history is more and more studied from an international angle. From other points of view, the new science of management has put greater stress on psychology; the bastard science of public relations has joined with socialist attitudes to stimulate the new discipline of sociology; and the computer is making heavy demands for mathematicians. All this and more the universities are trying to assimilate. Oxford is now offering joint degrees in economics and engineering, and in philosophy, psychology and politics. Cambridge, after much soul-searching, has established a new social science tripos. Warwick has ambitions to lead the field in mathematics. Nearly every university is studying some aspect of western Europe. Six universities are studying Latin America. University Centres set up under the Hayter Report are studying the countries and regions of Asia. The number of universities where Russian is studied is steadily increasing. Africa is almost as popular.

Fundamental changes are also taking place in university administration. Until 1914 universities were supported by private endowments and student fees. Today over 90% of university costs are paid for out of public funds. When public money was first given to universities, the University Grants Committee was set up expressly to act as a buffer between them and the government. The pendulum has now swung the other way. In the academic year 1967–68, £175m. was paid out to universities. Even though millionaires are now more plentiful than 'bishops in their shovel hats', that is quite a sizeable sum to come out of the public purse, and Members of Parliament, whose most important job is still to watch over government expenditure, are to be applauded rather than blamed for demanding close control over its use. The effect on the universities themselves, however, threatens to be catastrophic. They are not like armies, or navies, or post offices, or health services. They are intensely individual units, each of which has to pursue its own purpose in its own way if it is to give of its best to its students and to the general pursuit of knowledge. They are no more a social service than art or letters or sport, and if they are bureaucratised they will either wither and die or, which is worse in the long run, become permanently unfruitful.

This is the leading challenge to the British academic community today. It is new only in the modern context, for it has been posed, and successfully met, in other social contexts in earlier years. The fight for independence is a recurrent theme in the history of universities. There has always been some element in society seeking to dominate and control them. So far they have mostly been successful in beating off the threat. If they should ever finally lose the will to resist, another dark age will be on our doorsteps.

CHAPTER THREE

The world community of learning

The British universities can no more be understood in isolation than any one branch of knowledge can be fully comprehended other than in relation to the whole field of knowledge. One need not have an intimate understanding of the whole to have a working knowledge of the part, but one must be aware of the part's incompleteness and its dependence on its intellectual neighbours. The community of learning is world wide in an even deeper sense than is a Church. It has no Pope, Archbishop or Caliph to define its limits or prescribe a dogma. Scholars share nothing in common but a desire for knowledge. They can, and do, form factions and build up rivalries and enmities, but these disturbances are domestic to the world of learning and tend to dissolve on the disappearance of the protagonists. They are rarely, if ever, based on geographic or national considerations.

From the beginning, learning has been an international occupation. The earliest universities—Salerno, Bologna, Paris, Oxford, Prague— were no more national institutions than the MCC or the Royal & Ancient are confined to Marylebone or St Andrews. Each was a centre of learning, open to all comers, and both Masters and students would move from one to another with a freedom that has never been matched since the mediaeval world gave way to the nation state. It is a curious paradox that as means of communication have improved communication itself has become more difficult. There was greater freedom of movement when a man could travel no faster than a horse could gallop than there is in the days of the jet engine and the hovercraft.

Nevertheless, the world of learning has remained pre-eminently international both in spirit and in practice. It has to suffer under many deprivations in this respect. Frontier obstacles, economic obstacles, racial obstacles, ideological obstacles litter its path like a minefield. In spite of them, the people whose business is learning contrive to share, if not always their discoveries (for that might amount to high treason in this extraordinary world) at least their queries and their doubts. Above all, the world of learning offers constant asylum to its members. When the home situation gets too severe, the Einsteins, and many, many lesser

Einsteins, fly abroad and are welcomed. One of the more peculiar irrationalities besetting the minds of politicians is what is called the 'brain drain'. There is no such thing as a brain drain, only a brain expeller. Brains will always drift to the lands where academic inquiry is free. They will always fly from lands where efforts are made to control them. And the lands where academic inquiry is free are the great manufactories of brains. My own country, Scotland, is a case in point. We have exported brains for centuries and the home market has never suffered. We are also a country where a certain national pride has helped to keep our universities freer than most.

The academic community has a loyalty of its own, a sense of identity and common purpose that transcends frontiers and ideologies. In spite of the politicians, it has contrived to weave a world-wide net of inter-communication based partly on the printed word and increasingly on personal liaison. It is not only dons who travel. The habit is growing for students to spend a part of their undergraduate years in a university or universities abroad, or at any rate in hitch-hiking all over the Continent. All British universities have some foreign staff, and I imagine that this is true of every university everywhere. There are probably some Czechs in Moscow and some Albanians in China.

There are, according to *The World of Learning* (1971–72 edition), some 2,400 universities in the world. In Britain and Eire, 52; in western Europe, 203; in eastern Europe, 62; in the USSR, 49; in America north of Mexico, 1,285[1]; in Central and South America, 240; in the Middle East and the Mehgreb, 48; in Africa, 52; in Asia, 370; in Australasia, 21; in the Caribbean, 8; in the Pacific, 36. New universities are continually being established; these figures exclude many other institutions of higher education that have not yet reached university status. The figures show not only how large is the urge towards learning, but also how wide-spread.

The total number of university students, according to the latest UNESCO figures (1967–68), is 23·1 m., which is 0·07% of the estimated world population. The British student population in the same year was 232,137, which is 0·42% of the British population.

These are macro-statistics. If this were a textbook on higher education I would endeavour to work out such refinements as the number of foreign dons and students in British universities or the number of British dons and students in foreign universities, or the number of British graduates who hold degrees from universities in more than one country. It is sufficient to say that such numbers are substantial, and that

---

[1] This massive figure excludes innumerable other higher education institutions that elsewhere might qualify as universities.

the British community of learning has intimate links with similar communities overseas.

A brief survey of certain other regions might, however, help to give perspective to the picture. What follows does not attempt to do more than describe the university situation elsewhere in the barest detail.

Europe. The Dark Ages separated the centres of learning of Greece and Rome from the emergent universities of the Middle Ages. Only the tenuous link with the centres of Arabic learning and the long continuum of Talmudic studies joins them. The modern university system took root, as we shall see in the next chapter, in the twelfth and thirteenth centuries in Italy and France, and spread into Britain, Germany, the Low Countries, Spain and Scandinavia at varying degrees of speed. Africa, apart from the extreme north of the continent, remained without universities until very recent times. In Asia, learning was in the main confined to purely religious establishments. The New World acquired universities in the wake of colonisation. What is now eastern Europe but what was, as it still is, a part of Europe, began to acquire universities contemporaneously with Germany.

From their beginning, the British universities had strong links with the Continent. Oxford and Cambridge are of Parisian ancestry. The Scottish universities spring from France and Italy. This explains, in part, their different development, but it also illustrates the close relationship that has always bound all communities of learning into a single, even if very loose-knit, community. The mediaeval period was the great age for university foundation. First Salerno, then Bologna, then Paris and then, in a growing flood, come over seventy others, all within less than three centuries. There was, however, to be one significant difference between Britain and the Continent. In Britain the universities quickly won their freedom from external control; on the Continent they fell first under Church domination and then, for the most part, under the state. For centuries continental higher education has been a state preserve. It is only recently, in the last fifty years, that the British universities have had to surrender their autonomy.

Present conditions in the continental universities scarcely afford a recommendation for state control, and the same can be said of recent developments in Britain or, indeed, North America. But it is doubtful whether the system is at fault so much as the general social atmosphere which has led to one of those periodic revolts of youth against a changing world in which it is trying to find its place. Whatever the reason, the old tradition of learning remains, and it is fair to say that, in spite of modern difficulties, the European universities continue to fulfil their essential role of passing on knowledge and extending it. In no other continent is learning pursued with greater objectivity or success.

North America. The American university system began in colonial days, and has developed into a mixture of private foundations and state universities. The proportion of students to population is the highest in the world. We have already seen in Chapter One how a 'college education' was part of the American Dream, and how influential this was in spreading the urge towards higher education in Britain. The American universities, however, are very much *sui generis.* They owe something to their mediaeval European ancestors, but just as the mediaeval universities reflected the needs and pressures of the emergent civilisation that had given them birth, so their American counterparts reflect the expansive, ebullient panorama of the technocrat civilisation of the New World. In so far as they are enormous in size compared with British universities and put much less emphasis on close student/teacher relationships, they take after the continental European model; but their approach to scholarship is different as well. They have pioneered in many fields—international politics, linguistics and development economics are some examples—and their range of studies goes far beyond what, until very recently, was thought necessary in this country—ice-cream technology, for instance. But their most distinguishing feature is a meticulous concentration on detail. Research is brought down to such fine points of specialism that subjects that might rate an assistant lecturer elsewhere, here enjoy a Chair to themselves. It is probably due to the sheer weight of numbers. There are so many American seekers after Ph.Ds that there is scarcely a corner of Europe that will not yield one up, busily researching into the economics of Neapolitan taxi-drivers under the Mussolini regime or the bicycle trade in the Grand Duchy of Luxembourg at the turn of the century. Just as Profiles in the *New Yorker* go on and on and on about the most trivial details in the not very interesting lives of their subjects, so American university textbooks go on page after page about the more esoteric aspects of the point under discussion. There is nothing new under the sun. 'Precept upon precept, precept upon precept,' said the Prophet, 'line upon line, line upon line, here a little and there a little.' Many modern American students must echo his complaint.

One gets the impression that American academics have descended on the world of learning like a swarm of locusts, leaving it so parched and bare that they have had to find other outlets for their energies; perhaps this is why so many of them have turned to the more fruitful fields of government employment, speech writing for presidents, evaluating weapon systems, manning the government think-tanks and writing popularised sociology and psychology.

That is not to say that all American scholarship is inadequate. America has produced, and is producing, its fair share of the great scholars of the world; but it is also an outstanding example of the doctrine that 'more is worse'. All the same, links between the British and American communities of learning are close and fruitful. It is partly a matter of language, partly the generosity of American universities in offering visiting professorships and lectureships to British dons, but mostly a kind of academic 'special relationship' that reaches back to the days when the first American foundations were set up on British models.

Asia. The university, or seminary, was an integral part of Asian civilisations, as it must be of any civilisation, but it was at first wholly dominated by religion. It was the impact of the West that introduced the idea of secular study. Most of the universities in India and Pakistan owe their inspiration to Oxford and Cambridge, and have emerged as strangely oriental versions of them. The Indian mind is fashioned for metaphysical speculation, and schools of theology flourish, but they make provision for the arts and, particularly since independence, science and technology are being increasingly better taught. They have had to overcome great difficulties. In numbers they far exceeded what the traffic could bear; unemployed B.A.s piled up like a log jam, producing a body of intellectual discontent which made a major contribution to the expulsion of the British Raj. Most of all, they had to fight a grinding poverty which found its main reflection in a total inadequacy of books despite the herculean efforts of the Oxford University Press through its Indian branches. It would be fair to say that, since the transfer of power, the situation has improved under the twin benevolences of foreign aid and the pressures of industrialisation, but intercourse with Britain still remains largely one-way.

The University of Malaya, by contrast, is more clearly recognisable as a British foundation. It was a late arrival, but Malaya is a wealthy country and is less heavily overridden by spirituality than the subcontinent—two factors that have helped the university to achieve a western rather than an eastern image. It has many Chinese scholars on its staff and as the Chinese, like the Japanese, are highly susceptible to western influence, relations with western universities and the western publishing world are close.

As for China itself, very little can at this stage be said. The Chinese are an ancient people whose prowess in learning can be traced back beyond the beginnings of western learning in ancient Greece. There were no universities as we understand them. The desire to probe into reality was absent. In China, knowledge was formalised and transmitted but not greatly enlarged. Efforts were made by Europeans to establish

European-type universities, of which the American University in Shanghai was the most outstanding. It survived the second world war, and continued to exercise some degree of independence for several years after the establishment of the communist regime; nobody ever knew which members of its staff were paid by the original foundation, which by the communist government or by the CIA. The probability is that most of them drew three salaries and maintained an uneasy form of academic freedom in that way.

The latest edition of *The World of Learning* lists twenty-eight universities in China. Its guess is as good as anyone else's. The one thing of which we can be certain is that the new China has ambitions to rival the Japanese challenge to the West, in the academic field as much as in any other.

Japan, as one would expect, is largely dominated by American influence, and gives the same pride of place to higher education. When I mentioned to a colleague that Greater London Council officials had told me with a measure of awe that London already had three universities, he said, 'Tell them that Tokyo has 200.' This was a pardonable exaggeration; it does have over 38! Japan is the one non-Western country to have leaped across the gulf separating the 'undeveloped' from the 'developed' nations, and now bids fair to outstrip its former masters. It has exchanged the worship of its emperor for the worship of higher education. The best Japanese universities, like the best Japanese ships and motor cars, are wholly comparable to their Western equivalents, and as far as intercourse with American universities is concerned the language problem seems to present no serious barrier. Any American publisher of academic books will confirm that judgement.

Colonial Africa. Black Africa enjoys neither an ancient civilisation nor wealth. Its university system reflects both these lacks, not entirely to its own disadvantage. There is a certain virtue in being *tabula rasa*. Most, but not all, African universities were established during the colonial period. In British colonies they were designed on British lines; they were staffed initially by British academics, and aimed at tutoring for British degrees. A parallel situation existed in francophone Africa. Neither the Portuguese nor the Spanish were deeply interested in African higher education; nor, for that matter, were the Belgians. I believe it is correct to say that at the time of Congolese independence there was only one Congolese law graduate, and he had graduated from a Belgian university.

Today there are 50 African universities in former colonial territories. Of these, the most outstanding are the University of Sierra Leone, Makarere University in Uganda and the University of Ghana. The policy of 'Africanisation' is making progress in the universities, but probably to a lesser degree than in the African armies or civil service because dons enjoy less direct power than soldiers or bureaucrats. This has on the whole been helpful to African higher education. I hope that the Race Relations Board will not call me to order for that remark. Competent soldiers and competent bureaucrats can be turned out quite easily. Competent dons come more slowly and with greater difficulty. There is a growing number of African scholars, but they are still helped forward by the large numbers of Europeans who occupy important posts in their universities. Academic staffs are fashioned over generations, not within them.

There are two important points of interest about the African world of learning. The first is that the rest of the world is immensely interested in Africa. I once saw what claimed to be a directory of what are called 'africanists'. It was roughly half the size of the *Concise Oxford English Dictionary*. Perhaps half of those listed were Africans. Most of the remainder were Europeans or North Americans, very many of whom pursue their studies by going to teach in African universities. These universities thus enjoy an unfailing source of staff recruitment among non-African scholars, many of them of high competence.[1]

The second point of interest is that African universities show as much interest in African studies as Irish universities show in Irish studies. This is of course natural. English universities have a special interest in English history and English literature, but anyone who spent some time in Queen's, Belfast, or in Trinity College or University College, Dublin, will know what it is for a university to be obsessed by its country's past. It is a product of the emergence from colonialism. The newly free nation has to establish its identity. It is much easier for it to do so if it is at some geographical distance from its former governor. The Irish Sea is only a narrow strait, and memories of bondage are still strong enough to make Irish history and Irish folklore subjects of high academic importance. Makerere and Ibadan, Sierra Leone and Accra are all a long way from Whitehall, but they are still in the earliest stages of independence, and they suffer under the added strain of an inevitable sense of racial prejudice. If the African rulers are wise they will not press too strongly the africanisation of their universities; but our universities here at home do also have much to gain through continued close association with the African universities. They are still fresh and young, and these are qualities to be desired.

In South Africa, the universities have been longer established and

---

[1] It will be interesting, and possibly sad, to see what happens to Makerere now that President Amin has expelled its European teachers.

bear more resemblance to their English and Dutch counterparts, but their academic life is bedevilled by the problems of apartheid.

There is one constant factor common to all universities wherever they may be located: the love–hate relationship between students and staff. This is as common a phenomenon as Thurber's war between men and women. Peking, Moscow, Nanterre, York, Santa Barbara or Frankfurt in the twentieth century; Salerno in the twelfth century; Paris, Oxford and Prague through the whole of their long histories—the record is one of conflict.

One should not make too much of it. Friction is the best method of sharpening a knife, and the academic knife needs to be keen if it is to carve its way into the hidden realms of knowledge. The very similarity of academic problems throughout the world and throughout the ages is in itself a beacon of hope. It is a sign that the world of learning has an intrinsic unity both in space and in time. It is this unity that makes membership of a university membership of a world-wide community transcending the pettiness of day-to-day national affairs.

CHAPTER FOUR

The academic background

The British university system, in so far as it can be called a system at all, is no more the product of the last twenty-five years than the British Parliament is the product of the Reform Act of 1832 and its subsequent embellishments. Its roots lie deep in the Middle Ages and far beyond that; like the individual, each university reflects the hereditary influence of its own genes, the determining features of which took shape long before the point to which most of us can trace back our own ancestries.

It is fashionable to date the beginnings of the modern western-type university to the spate of foundations that followed on the establishment of the medical school of Salerno in the eleventh century. The real roots are even more remote. The Dark Ages that separated the mediaeval from the ancient world were not completely devoid of learning, though the best of it was located outside Europe. These were the centuries that saw the flowering of Arab civilisation and the main development of the Talmudic studies of the Jewish people, two streams of intellectual adventure which intermingled in Alexandria to produce, if not a direct link, at least a somewhat tenuous chain of association between the centres of Roman scholarship and Plato's Academy on the one hand, and the first stirrings of Europe's Renaissance on the other. The Christian monasteries kept the flame of learning alight after their fashion, but the Jews and Arabs used it to illuminate new fields of study, and it was primarily through them that European learning was set back on the road to recovery. We have been taught to believe that there was some kind of fortuitous rediscovery of the works of Aristotle that triggered off the revival of learning. What actually happened is that the Jews carried Greek philosophy to the receptive minds of the nascent civilisation of the Near East, and that it was from the Arab world that it returned to western Europe.

The process of learning suffers its setbacks, but it is continuous. It is coterminous with the development of civilisations. When a civilisation fails it leaves shreds and patches of its learning to be picked up by its successors, just as a Jowett or an Einstein when he dies leaves some elements of his achievement to those who follow him. European universities began in the Athenian Agora where Socrates became an outstanding teacher. There was no more organisation, probably less, than there is at Speaker's Corner in Hyde Park, but there was a free forum for discussion and people came to it, not consciously to learn but to hear what others had to say and to argue with them. These were primitive days, and the ideas put forward were primitive in terms of today's sophistication of thought. The Agora was not a teaching establishment for the young; it was an exchange mart for ideas among grown men. It was, nevertheless, a place of learning where people could sharpen their wits and probe below the surface of their daily lives. It was in that milieu that Socrates emerged as one of the most original thinkers of all time. He saw more clearly than the establishment of his day and they executed him for his pains. It was the West's first example of the clash between freedom of thought and established political power.

The elimination of Socrates was a purely physical achievement. His ideas were taken up and developed by Plato, who established, in his Academy the prototype of the modern seat of learning. It was a centre to which seekers after truth could come to find guidance through the darkness of man's ignorance of the material world. From it arose the schools of Greek philosophy that were to have such a profound influence over future generations, not least over St Paul as he toiled over the building of the Christian Church. They not only developed the concept of speculation and learning as the twin sources of human advance, but also created a mechanism by means of which each generation succeeded to a higher, firmer platform of knowledge than its predecessors had enjoyed. Rome took over when Greece failed, but its form of learning had an emphasis of its own. Its main strengths lay in technology and law, the world of practical accomplishment and the social sciences rather than that of metaphysical speculation. It was directed more towards empire-building than to the conquest of knowledge for its own sake. Its memorials were roads and law, engines of war and the arts of government. By comparison with Greece it added little to the concept of the university.

While Arabian civilisation developed Europe plunged deeper and deeper into its Dark Ages, a period of political chaos and intellectual doldrums. The monasteries kept the principles and theology of Christianity alive but made no great contribution to the advancement of learning. They also kept alive an ovum of civilisation, but it had to wait for refertilisation from elsewhere before a new advance could be made.

It was natural that this should have taken place in Italy. In Spain, where Moslem and Christian were still at war, the barrier was at its most impenetrable. There is no immediate give and take on the march between two civilisations. It was from Africa, according to semi-historical tradition, that Scipio Africanus brought to Italy, geographically speaking the closest point to Alexandria, the first rudiments of the new learning. He brought his knowledge of the medicine of Hippocrates and Galen to Salerno, and students flocked from all over Europe to the first rudimentary medical school of western civilisation. 'We may smile at this mediaeval medicine,' H. A. L. Fisher wrote in his *History of Europe*. 'It was combined with astrology. It was prefaced by a careful study of the writings of Aristotle. Yet this is the principal root from which the science of the Renaissance was destined to grow.'

Salerno was followed shortly by Bologna which specialised, as might be expected in the homeland of Roman civilisation, in law; and a little later by Paris, where theology was the main subject of study. Thereafter universities began to spring up throughout what is now western Europe, from Cracow in the east to Lisbon in the west, from St Andrews and Uppsala in the far north to Catania in Sicily. Their patrons were the Popes or local royalties. Their organisation was loose, and varied from place to place, and from the very beginning struggles for control emerged —between teachers and students, between the university and the Church, between the university and the temporal power. The history of the mediaeval universities is a confused but fascinating chronicle of a process of trial and error, pressure and counter-pressure, leading to the emergence of a new and significant social institution.

The influence of universities, in dragging the western world up out of the Dark Ages through the chaos of the mediaeval world to the point in the sixteenth and seventeenth centuries where modern history can be said to have begun, was no less profound than that of statesmen and soldiers. This work was crucial to the whole process of creating the infinitely more sophisticated understanding of man's environment, both philosophic and material, that underlies western civilisation as we know it today. But for the universities' unremitting search after knowledge, conducted at first haphazardly but in later years with increasing systematisation, the West would never have been able to mould itself into a coherent whole and extend its influence over virtually the whole globe. I am not thinking primarily of the natural sciences, though advances in these have been the dominant feature of the last century, but rather of the development of the techniques and methodologies of study. As the universities grew into established institutions and new foundations came in to swell the total of academic effort, the community of learning slowly began to develop, building up the dexterity of mind and method needed to probe further into reality and thus to open up new fields of enterprise to the creative urge. Society, as distinct from the individual, had acquired a prehensile thumb.

By the middle of the nineteenth century the academic community had developed a character of its own. Practice differed from university to university and from country to country. Each institution tended to follow its own star. There was interference enough when established values were threatened or whenever statesmen could sense an advantage from it, but the academics were inclined to fight back, and were as often as not successful. All the same, the sense of coherence tended to dominate over diversity. Neither students nor their masters were confined to a single base. Just as today they ride the airlines in search of new sources and new outlets, so in these early formative years they made their way slowly and painfully from centre of learning to centre of learning eager to broaden their own knowledge or enter into discussions or disputations with their equals or betters. Tentacles of information spread out like a nervous sytem, linking Oxford with Paris, with Heidelburg, with Buda, with Basle, with Prague. Travelling scholars were to be met with on the roads. 'Indeed we are not gentlemen,' one of two wayfarers protested to Montaigne's servant who had accosted them as such. 'He is a grammarian and I am a logician.'

Thus, gradually, a sense of common identity emerged, giving the universities of the western tradition a sufficiently similar outlook to make each comprehensible to the rest. They were not homogeneous, nor did they follow slavishly the same intellectual fashions, but they shared a common intellectual approach, talked a common intellectual language, pursued a common ultimate aim and welcomed interchange as much as they indulged in rivalry. Their rivalries were, indeed, one of the main factors that held them together. The blood-brothership of the golfing or sailing worlds would be a pale reflection of the reality were it not for their competitive opportunities.

The university community of the 1840s had certain general characteristics. It was hierarchic, with student and master occupying clearly defined places. Among the masters, the concept of professorial dignity and control was universally accepted, but a constitutional form of government, varying in detail from place to place, had been developed to regulate relations between faculties and between disciplines, to protect the community's rights *vis-à-vis* the outside world and to make rules for its internal governance. Each university regarded itself as something apart from the society in which it lived in so far as it was dedicated to the pursuit of truth rather than to the general scramble for wealth, and claimed, by virtue of that distinction, the right to run its own affairs. This concept of academic freedom, which was directed not only against the state but against any power that might offer interference, was of course only partially effective; the universities were the prisoners both of their own traditions and of the general mores of the society in which they had their place. Nearly all were religious foundations and accepted the spiritual, if not the temporal, authority of the parent Church. Equally, they accepted the current views on the position of women and the more or less Pauline concept of the relation between master and pupil. They were monastic and authoritarian, but within that traditional and social framework they claimed and exerted the right to independence. On its side, the state was apt to let them go their own way, though in times of civil war it was inevitable that they should become involved. In the modern world of collective thought and changing social values, academic freedom has become the subject of a complex and widespread debate— but its roots lie in the death of Socrates.

Tradition also dictated the subjects for study. As we have seen, the mediaeval universities came into being largely to meet a demand for doctors, lawyers and churchmen, the three most important elements in the social structure of the times. Later, as understanding became more sophisticated, they found they could only study these subjects in depth if they moved on to related subjects such as the nature and meaning of language, the discipline of logical thinking, philosophical speculation on the problem of good and evil and on the nature of reality. This last brought them to study the physical structure of matter (in Scotland physics is still called natural philosophy), anatomy, astronomy, the qualities of the vegetable world. Such was their early frontier, but the continent that lay beyond it was indescribably more vast than even Galileo or Copernicus could have realised (as, one might add in parenthesis, is the continent across the frontier occupied by the academics of today). Social pressures, which at most times are traditional rather than adventurous, urged them to concentrate mainly on what are now called the arts. Theology and law remained 'musts', but moral philosophy, grammar, logic, rhetoric and history helped to illuminate them. Physics and astronomy, too, were respectable in so far as they helped the study of theology. It took a long time to dissociate chemistry from magic and devilry, and when medicine began to call for human dissection tradition rose in revolt; the divine form was not a fit subject for practical experiment. This prejudice lasted into the nineteenth century, though by then it had become the province of a die-hard minority. Traces of it are still found. The most significant early advances in the natural sciences were made outside the university world, and it was not until the nineteenth century that science became a primary object of academic study.

An acceptance of the importance of technology came even later.

Working with the hands was not considered a suitable subject for clerks and gentlemen until long after the Industrial Revolution had put technical skills in the forefront of social needs. Such skills were taught at first in mechanics' institutes attended in the main by the sons of the working class. They were the forerunners of the modern technical institute and polytechnic, but also the roots from which sprang many of the great civic universities. It soon became apparent that technology was too closely linked with the burgeoning scientific academic disciplines for it to be pursued separately as a minor, less important field of study, but the resistance of the arts world was strong, and it was not until late in the century that the majestic university engineering schools began to take on their modern form.[1]

It is only quite recently that serious efforts have been made to bridge the arts/science gap, and it has taken place mainly in the newest of universities, Sussex in particular. As late as 1970 a distinguished classicist, on mentioning the Department of Education and Science, added in mischievous parenthesis: 'a significant and profound distinction!' That was 'donnishness' at its best—or worst—but it also represented a hangover from an earlier age, not a theme of current thought. Most dons today accept the basic unity of all branches of study, and the need for all arts students to understand something of scientific principles.

Bridging the gap is, however, more easily imagined than accomplished. The lines between the two branches of study had been allowed to become firm and unbending—arts and social sciences for a general education, the natural sciences for specialism. The 'significant and profound distinction' contained more than a grain of truth. The efforts now being made to close the gap come mainly from the arts side, and they do not always stimulate a reciprocal enthusiasm.

Since the 1940s a new branch of study has been building up in the universities, variously termed the history of science or the philosophy of science or, more generally, the history and philosophy of science. It was originally the product of the philosophers, who have increasingly become poachers in other disciplines. University syllabuses bristle with courses on such subjects as the philosophy of history, of education, of religion, of mathematics, of linguistics, of psychology. It is what might be termed, *pace* the philosophers, applied philosophy as distinct from pure philosophy—ethics, aesthetics, epistomology, logic and metaphysics. These latter-day philosophic studies owe the vigour with which they are pursued

---

[1] As late as the early years of the twentieth century another traditional prejudice still clung to the teaching of technology. A lady who at that time was the only woman student reading engineering at Cambridge tells how the demonstrators used to ignore her presence as they came round the class.

to the growing philosophic conviction that no subject can be studied seriously without the benefit of philosophic analysis. Two subjects, however, have since Aristotle been the particular external grazing grounds of the philosophers—politics and science. The schools of politics have more or less accepted their provenance. The scientists have not, though it is difficult to name any one of the leading modern philosophers from Descartes to Russell who have not delved deeply into scientific questions. The new courses on the history and philosophy of science are taken mainly by arts students. Science students are discouraged by their teachers from having anything to do with them. 'My students have too much else to learn to be able to waste their time on the history of error,' one chemistry professor said recently, oblivious of the high probability that in the twenty-first century he will be accused of teaching error himself.

University science today enforces a narrow specialism. Given the undoubted demand for specialists this is probably inevitable—it is in tune with the materialist ethos of modern society—but it is questionable whether it is a Good Thing in the long run. The scientist needs to understand something of the wider range of experience outside his own specialism, especially at a time when the fragmentation of research is such that the boundaries of specialism become narrower with each advance. The process is, moreover, reaching downwards into schools, where specialisation begins at an increasingly early age. The head of the humanities department of a university that grew out of one of the technical colleges once told me that most of his students had studied nothing apart from mathematics and science since the age of fourteen or even earlier—no history, no literature, no elementary philosophy. It was, he said, like being driven back to scratch. He was tempted to make Lamb's *Tales from Shakespeare* a set book.

This clear-cut division cannot be acceptable for long, even less from the social than from the academic point of view. There is no immediate blame for it to be handed out. It is rooted in organic growth, not in the malefactions of the present. If I seem to have laboured the point, it is because I want to emphasise that the university of today is not the product of its academic staff for the time being, but of a long process of development that imposes its own rules on the present. There is just as much original sin in an institution as in an individual—perhaps more, because so many individuals have contributed to its growth.

There is, however, another entirely different aspect of the past's mortmain over the university system of today. It is no less important for being administrative rather than academic. As we have seen, most of the mediaeval universities were founded on the authority of the Church or the local temporal power, and their relationship with these authorities became more and more uneasy as each university developed a personality and strength of its own. Under these stresses, the continental universities developed along different lines from the British. The reasons are to be found in the social and political differences between the two types of polity. Firm, centralised government developed earlier in England than on the Continent, and although it might be thought that this would help to place the universities more firmly under the control of the state, the effect was precisely the opposite. On the Continent, the instabilities and uncertainties of political life forced the universities to seek out protectors and to identify themselves with some outside power, with the result that state-supported universities have become the norm south and east of the English Channel. In England, where the king's writ ran ever more effectively from the days of Henry II, universities were able to organise themselves free from the fear of takeover by ambitious local barons. They were also helped by the Reformation, which broke the power of the Church, and the dissolution of the monasteries, through which they fell heir to much of the monasteries' wealth and found themselves well able to pay their own way without having to seek subventions from the royal exchequer. The situation was at first somewhat different in Scotland, but after the Union of the Crowns the Scottish universities began to settle more into the English mould.

British universities, therefore, developed under a tradition of independence while those on the Continent developed as state institutions, their association with the state becoming closer as government became more firmly established. This distinction was to produce a curious reversal of position in the present century. When Britain's civic universities were established in the nineteenth century, they had to fit in with the general pattern and find means of paying for themselves. Though they received some support, largely indirect, from local authorities, they received little or none from central government funds. The establishment of new universities was essentially a private matter, with local magnates bearing the brunt of the cost. This feature of our university system ran right through until the second world war. Breaches were made in the principle after 1918, as the growing cost of scientific and technological teaching and research outstripped their otherwise ample resources, but a mechanism was devised to protect their independence. The University Grants Committee was established to receive and evaluate university requests for funds, and then applied to the Treasury for a grant equivalent to the total amount it felt should be provided. This grant was made to the Committee (not to individual universities), which passed it on in such proportions as it felt most suitable, and the funds thus made available were then left to the universities to spend at their own discretion. In effect, the Committee acted as a buffer between universities and the government; there were no direct dealings between the two principals. Once they had received their grants, the universities continued to administer them with the same freedom they enjoyed over their private funds. The government was in much the same position as a private benefactor.

Meanwhile, the continental universities continued to protect their independence by other means. As state institutions, they had always been largely dependent on state money, but the lines of the relationship had hardened back in the early days long before collectivist theory had coupled state support with detailed state control. Academic freedom came to be accepted as the norm, and was buttressed by devices such as the life tenure of professors, a kind of 'parson's freehold' that enabled them to hold their positions indefinitely until they decided to give them up of their own accord. While this removed them from the authority of the state, it also led to a hardening of the arteries of the academic community, and has been one of the main factors in the European universities' time of troubles in the late 1960s.

On the Continent, as in Britain, the higher education explosion of the post-second world war period caught the academic community off balance—but for different reasons. On the Continent, the universities were entrenched behind a fortress wall of tradition and convention, but were nevertheless flooded by vast hordes of new students with whom they were largely unable to cope. Neither staff, lecture halls nor libraries were adequate. New students, lacking advice as to procedure, had to find their own way round. Many would never even meet their professors during the whole of their university lives. In Bonn as late as 1968 there were stories of students having to queue up outside the library at seven in the morning in the hope of being in time to lay hands on the books they needed. The grounds for student discontent were overt and largely unanswerable. Improvements are being made, especially in Germany, but the legacy of the past still lies heavy on the present.

In Britain the consequences have been quite different. The old system has been largely swept away, unable to withstand the joint pressures of expansion and inflation. It depended on economic independence, artificially sustained through the University Grants Committee between the wars. During these middle years the amount of government money channelled into the university chests was comparatively small. In 1939, it amounted to no more than £2·22 m. Thirty years later it was £200·31 m., an outstanding example of the Marxian axiom that there is a point at which an increase in quantity produces a change in quality.

With such immense sums of public money involved the University Grants Committee has come to perform a new function: instead of being a buffer between university and state, it has become a mechanism for channelling the requirements of a paymaster government down to the recipients of aid. In 1929 its staff was five. By 1969 it numbered 107, an increase wildly out of proportion to the increase in the numbers of students and academic staff.

This is a contentious subject. There is a powerful school of thought, by no means unrepresented within the academic community itself, which believes that universities should be no less subject to public control than schools. Against it stand those who believe that no university can fulfil its function unless it enjoys the full right to manage its own affairs. This is not the place to attempt to unravel this argument. I mention it simply because it is impossible to understand the present university atmosphere without knowing the nature of this often bitter debate. The crux of it lies in the fact that, whereas the continental universities became linked with the state at a time when government control lay comparatively lightly on such institutions, the collapse of the old British system coincided almost precisely with the growth of the belief that it is the duty of government to control every last aspect of the educational process. In other words, the future of the universities has become the core of a national debate on the fundamental nature of government, education is becoming a major battleground for the politicians. The effect of this on the academic community is only now beginning to show itself. It lies at the root of many of the recent university troubles, and it will almost certainly prove an increasing source of disarray in the years ahead.

CHAPTER FIVE

The organisation of learning

Like any other social institution, a university is dependent on its ability to organise itself in a manner that will enable it to carry out its purposes effectively. It is a community of individuals, rarely less than 3,000 of them, who must find ways of working together in a fair degree of harmony if their widely varying but closely linked aims are not to be thwarted by dissension and anarchy. Their individual interests are multifarious and diverse, their points of contact often seemingly remote. The student of nuclear physics and the learned researcher into early Cyrillic palaeography have no obvious or immediate links with each other; nor does the demonstrator in the biology laboratory with the professor of English literature. Yet they are all a part of the chain of learning and discovery. The problem of the university (or the *studium generale*, to give it its ancient, and in this context more revealing, title) is to reconcile the aims and ambitions of all its members within an enduring and self-governing framework. That calls for a sophistication of organisation far beyond the rough and ready methods of industrial empires or even governments. Frontiersmen cannot afford the luxury of fundamental division.

There are five main facets of the problem: to reconcile conflict between student and teacher, between teacher and researcher, between administrator and teacher, between the teachers themselves and between the university and the neighbourhood in which it is situated. The university that can achieve all these aims is likely to be successful. Failure in any one ultimately means the failure of the whole enterprise.

As a self-governing community within society, and with responsibilities to society, a university must abide by the rules that society lays down for its conduct. Each university is bound by its foundation document which, in the case of the mediaeval universities, usually took the form of a papal decree or a charter from the local temporal power. Most of the universities in Britain today are bound by a Royal Charter, and all the new universities that have been established recently have a similar legal base. The charter grants the university the right to confer degrees, and lays down in a series of statutes the essential features of its organisation.

That, however, is only the beginning of the matter. Within that framework the university must make its own detailed rules, normally called regulations or ordinances, which govern its academic structure and internal relations between its members.

In Britain, a Royal Charter is granted by the monarch on the advice of his or her Privy Council. In the nineteenth century, when universities were few in number, such charters were granted reluctantly and only after a long period of trial and error. It took fifty years to obtain a charter for the University of Manchester. More recently charters have been granted more easily, but at first not until after the new institution had served a probationary period as a university college attached for examination purposes and general supervision to one of the existing universities. This practice extended even to the colonies. Fourah Bay College in Sierra Leone, for instance, served its apprenticeship as a college of the University of Durham. The situation has changed completely now that it has become government policy to increase the number of universities, and while still nominally granted on Privy Council advice, a Royal Charter is effectively a creation of the government of the day. This is natural enough, considering that it is paid for out of public funds. What would be the response to an application from a group of private citizens prepared to finance it themselves is an issue that will soon be tested, it is hoped, when the petition from the Independent University Planning Board comes up for consideration.

The Charter is the product of negotiation between the sponsors of the university, its first office holders and the committee of the Privy Council charged with the duty of advising the monarch. If the sponsor is the government, there is only a small area for discussion. If, on the other hand, the petition to the monarch were to come from a group of private individuals, the Privy Council would have to satisfy itself on a number of points. Are the sponsors reliable and responsible people? Are their proposals for the constitutional and academic structure of the university sound? Does the proposal enjoy strong local support? Is there a need for a university in the neighbourhood proposed? Are the financial provisions adequate? All these and other factors have to be taken into consideration.

The Charter, when it is finally granted, takes the form of a long and detailed legal document. Its purpose is to ensure that the new institution will be so designed and so organised as to make it a worthy addition to the community of learning. After reciting the circumstances that have led to the petition being presented, it formally founds and constitutes the new institution, and lists in detail the powers it confers on the body corporate. These vary from the power to grant degrees (or to deprive people of degrees already granted!) to the right to own and manage property and work in association with other universities. The powers are not as wide as those normally granted to a new limited liability company in its Articles of Association, but they usually include authority to do anything that a university might reasonably have to do in order to carry out its purposes.

It then goes on to describe in very broad outline the methods by which the university shall be governed. First, it lists the principal offices and the main organs of government, usually a court, a council, a senate, a convocation and an assembly, and indicates the part each will play in the running of the institution. It usually prescribes the broad outlines of the academic structure, and it will also confer the power to make ordinances for the detailed day-to-day management of the university's affairs. The real meat of the charter, however, is to be found in the attached 'schedules'. One schedule will list the members of the sponsoring committee who have petitioned for the grant of the charter. Another will name the first office-holders, the first members of the university court and, very probably, the first deans of the various faculties or schools of study into which the university is divided. Finally come the statutes. These are the effective governing instrument and they define in close detail the constitutional methods by which the work of the university shall be organised. They define membership of the university, set out the procedure by which ordinances are to be made, and regulate the respective powers of the various organs of government, the manner of appointment, dismissal or retirement of staff and, in more detail nowadays than in the past, the organisation and rights of the student body. They are drafted by skilled constitutional lawyers, and in addition to their intended purpose provide a happy hunting ground for any barrack-room lawyers who happen to be members of the university.

The Charter is obviously vital. If it is not well drafted, the whole future of the institution can be prejudiced. Much care therefore goes into its preparation; it is doubtful if a sound charter could be produced in under a year of reasonably concentrated work, even when the government is the effective sponsoring committee. There is no such thing as a university die that can be used over and over again to stamp out similar institutions as a machine stamps out spare parts for a car. Each university is an individual entity, reflecting the neighbourhood where it is located and the particular ideas of its original senior office-holders and staff. One has only to glance over the most recent charters, from Sussex to the New University of Ulster, to see how widely they differ in detail and emphasis.

Once a charter has been granted the real work of setting up a university begins. The vice-chancellor and his senior academic staff have already been appointed. They must first appoint additional staff, and then set about drafting the internal rules of the institution in the manner defined in the Charter. They have probably made a beginning on these tasks before the Charter has been granted. In the nineteenth century the university had to show its paces before a charter was granted, but in the rush and tumble of today, when founding universities is rather like striking matches (with the government fulfilling the triple role of striker, match and matchbox) the whole process is telescoped, and the Charter usually precedes or follows fast on the first intake of students. An exception was the New University of Ulster. The acute political problems afflicting that ill-starred part of the United Kingdom ensured that argument over the charter was continuing long after the university had opened its doors, and it did not finally receive the Royal Seal until a few days before the first degrees were due to be awarded.

The creation of a new university, whether publicly or privately sponsored, is an immensely exciting adventure, particularly for the first senior dons, who are offered the chance of putting into effect theories of higher education that have been smothered by the inertia of older institutions. Whatever the individual results may have been, the proliferation of new universities in the 1960s has brought a new breath of life into the British academic community. It has provided opportunities for experiment in what was tending to become a rigid and stratified profession, and if some of the experiments have failed, as a proportion of all experiments must, they have nevertheless helped to break down an endemic resistance to change. The established universities have been forced to take a new look at their own methods.

A university must be organised to fulfil two functions, teaching and research. In one sense they are antipathetic: research is concerned with extending the frontiers of knowledge, which can easily become an ivory tower occupation; teaching is a matter of providing most of the students with a background of existing knowledge and a general discipline of mind-training that will help them in later life. In fact, the two strands are indissoluble. Teaching without research becomes a mere matter of instruction; a university must keep itself up at the frontier if it is to give its students a real love of learning. Research without teaching, though it can be immensely rewarding—as many a pure research institute has proved—is apt to become imprisoned in its own specialism; the chief characteristic of a university is breadth of interest. Ideally, therefore, a university should make equal provision for both functions. In practice, however, the emphasis has to be placed on the teaching side. Students are numerically much the largest element in the community and their needs must be met. Most of them will leave on graduation; only a small proportion are preparing for higher degrees or doctorates. The university must, therefore, have a broad teaching base, tapering up in pyramid fashion to areas of rare research where a small number of graduate students join their teachers in exploring the frontier. But at the same time provision must be made for undergraduates to learn something of the importance and methodology of research work, so that they leave not simply 'stuft with learning' but with the habit of inquiry and its techniques firmly implanted in their minds.

No university today can cover the whole field of learning with equal success. An early decision must therefore be made as to the areas in which it hopes to excel. Excellence is a key word in the academic community, the aim which all university planners hold or should hold in view. Each university has its own list of excellencies, some of them topping all the others. Every university, however good it may be in all subjects, is outshone in some spheres by its rivals. Nevertheless, while it may seek to scale certain peaks, a university must teach a wide variety of disciplines. Only the most specialised can be excluded entirely, but there are many that need to be taught only at a lower level. The precise distribution of effort can only be determined after the main goals have been decided. What is important is that the student should be offered the opportunity not just to study a single subject in depth, but to study it in relation to other branches of knowledge.

In most modern universities there are two main methods of dividing up the field of learning—by faculties or by schools of study. Faculties group together cognate disciplines; the traditional divisions are into the arts, social sciences, law, theology, medicine, mathematics and natural sciences, though the last of these is often subdivided into engineering, chemistry, the biological sciences, physics, the applied sciences or some other aspect of scientific or technological study. Arts usually embraces classics, modern languages, philosophy, history, English language and literature, and archaeology. In some universities it includes geography, economics and mathematics, though elsewhere these may find their places respectively in science or social science, or even in individual faculties of their own. The social sciences usually embrace politics, sociology, psychology, law, anthropology, social administration, and sometimes economics, and economic and social history. The scientific faculties deal in more precise fields of study, and are all the more easily defined.

The object of the faculty system is to offer the student a particular area of study in which all the courses provided have obvious links with each other. The division into schools of study, on the other hand, is designed to offer a very wide-ranging choice of subject within a particular field. Thus, Essex has a School of Comparative Studies in which various countries or regions can be studied and compared from every aspect—literary, historical, philosophical, social, economic, ethnological, geographical; while Lancaster offers a School of Environmental Studies which embraces everything from the problems of new towns to the influence of climate on social organisation. The faculty system is usually to be found, with notable exceptions, in the old-established universities, while the schools system belongs in the main to the post-war foundations. It is the new look in academic organisation and its emergence may well turn out to be a turning point in academic practice. Changes in the academic world are slow, and it will be a long time before we shall know whether the new fashion has developed into a firm tradition.

Whichever method is adopted, the purpose is to provide an administrative and academic framework through which the business of learning can be given organisation and direction, and studies pursued with the necessary degree of breadth and flexibility. A single discipline, such as history or philosophy or geography, may well find itself a part of two or more faculties or schools, providing each with courses designed to serve its own special purposes. Thus, the head of a department of history may serve on the boards of the faculty of arts and the faculty of social sciences, offering courses of straight history for arts and of social or economic history for social sciences. Similarly a department of philosophy, in addition to the courses leading to an Honours degree in philosophy, may offer courses on the philosophy of sociology, education or psychology for the social scientists. Geography can serve the arts, social sciences or natural sciences in equal measure. Where the division is into schools of study and not into faculties the spread can be even wider, since the division is not between cognate disciplines but between purposes of study. Thus in Lancaster the School of Environmental Studies draws on an immense variety of disciplines ranging from archaeology and ancient history to physics and ecology.

The modern tendency is away from the old idea of self-sufficient departments each specialising in its own discipline. When I went up to Oxford in 1929, I told the Senior Tutor of my college that I wanted to read law and history. He replied firmly that I must read one or the other, and my three years were spent in the study of law. Such history as I learned came from desultory, undirected reading on the side. That would not happen in any of the new universities, where the emphasis is deliberately placed on interdisciplinary studies. In some of them the very word 'department' is expressly regarded as a dirty word, a kind of atavistic survival from the dark academic ages of forty years ago. Like most reformers and experimentalists, these modern dons tend to overstate their case. Even the universities in the vanguard still find it necessary to have a professor of each of the traditional disciplines, and to offer degrees in each of them. The difference between a department of history and a Chair of history is more verbal than real.

Nor are interdisciplinary studies as modern as their sponsors like to make out. Mediaeval students studied the Trivium and the Quadrivium.[1] The Cambridge Tripos offers considerable breadth of study. At Oxford, Greats and Modern Greats were essentially interdisciplinary in character. Except in the vocational disciplines like medicine, law, theology and the applied sciences, there is a necessary overspill of interest that must be taken into account, and even in vocational education there is much to be gained from acquiring some understanding of other approaches to the problem of knowledge.

The chief danger of interdisciplinary studies is that of fragmentation. C. E. Montague, in one of his critical essays, said he would much rather have a small freehold at the foot of Parnassus than shooting rights over the whole mountain. The academic Jack-of-all-trades has rarely studied a single subject in depth, though that is essential to lasting academic achievement. The problem is to strike a balance between too narrow a specialisation and too wide a range of interest. A main function of the governing bodies of faculties or schools is to ensure that this balance is properly kept.

An important aspect of academic organisation is the admissions policy by which students are selected. In many continental countries no properly qualified candidate can be rejected, one of the principal reasons for student overcrowding with all its attendant evils. In Britain the number of places available is limited to what the university succeeds in persuading the UGC it can handle effectively on the funds made available, and since the total number of such places is far below the number who qualify, there are many disappointments. At the time of writing, something like 20,000 qualified applicants each year fail to get to a university at all. The alternatives available to solve the problem are (a) to build more universities or enlarge existing ones while maintaining current standards, which, coupled with the policy of paying the cost out of public funds, would put an intolerable strain on the Exchequer; (b) to adopt the continental system which would almost certainly involve a catastrophic lowering of standards and would meet with the strongest opposition from the academic profession; (c) to insist on a raising of the staff/student ratio, which would equally stir up opposition, or to squeeze

---

[1] The Trivium included grammar, rhetoric and logic; the Quadrivium comprised arithmetic, music, geometry and astronomy. They were known together as the seven liberal arts.

a normal Honours degree into two years which would almost certainly reduce its value; or finally (d) to upgrade other institutions, such as polytechnics or colleges of education, to university status which, unless they were provided with the necessary additional facilities, would be no more than a confidence trick. There is also, of course, the Open University, but in spite of the undoubted merits of that interesting experiment, it is idle to suppose that a university worth the name can be established without some form of communal life and close personal contact between teacher and taught. It is improbable that the continental system will be adopted here, but efforts are being made along the lines of the other methods. A halt seems to have been called to the foundation of new universities, but existing ones are being enlarged as rapidly as funds permit; the UGC has already put forward proposals for a raising of the staff/student ratio and the reorganisation of syllabuses; and plans seem to be in hand to upgrade other institutions. But it is doubtful whether all these measures taken together will do much more than keep pace with the predicted increase of qualified applicants over the next decades, and leave the shortfall in available places as bad as or even worse than it already is. There are, of course, the possibilities of raising the standard of qualification or making the universities fee-paying institutions, but these are political hot potatoes that none of the parties seems willing to handle.

The universities themselves, therefore, remain the final arbiters of who shall or shall not be admitted, a situation not without merit if one accepts the fact that they are communities where communal lives depend on the individual quality of the members. Each has its own procedures for deciding on the selection of students, but they all look for roughly the same qualities—a proved ability for study, a motivation towards learning, a suitable personality and an appropriate choice of subject. In addition to these individual qualities, they have to pay attention to what is called the student mix. They try to preserve a reasonable balance between men and women, to find room for a number of mature students who have already spent some time out in the world earning their living, and also to include a number of students from overseas. Since their main purpose is not simply to shove undergraduates through on a conveyor belt but to produce successful graduates who will reflect credit on the institution, they set their standards well above the minimum, so that the practical result is to establish a higher standard than the minimum required by law.

Securing a university place is by no means easy. Until 1939 it was a comparatively simple matter, provided one could afford the fees. Though the number of available places was small, the number of candidates was miniscule in comparison with today's. Only the more able school-leavers were urged to go on to university, and the number who applied simply because their parents were rich enough to send them was small. Graduates almost invariably went into the professions, the Church or the Civil Service, or remained to establish their careers in the academic world. Very few went into business or industry. Nowadays business and industry absorb the bulk of graduates so that the acquisition of a degree has become one of the main gateways to success in these fields. The flood of applicants has become such a torrent that the universities would be overwhelmed if a means of canalising it had not been found. In 1961 the Universities Central Council for Admission (UCCA) was established. All applications must now be made through it, on an official application form which sets out full personal details of age, parents, education, 'O' and 'A' level qualifications and any other relevant details, and then lists in order of preference the first six universities of choice, together with the subjects it is wished to study. Copies are sent immediately to the universities of first choice, where they are winnowed through, some rejected at first sight, others set aside for further consideration and probably for interview. A rejected applicant is sent on to the university of second choice, and so on down the line. Total rejection is not final. An unsuccessful candidate can try again the following year, having used the interval to improve his qualifications. Nevertheless, the number who never succeed is high. The clever completion of the UCCA application form is obviously one of the keys to success. The applicant must know what he is about and show that he is clear as to his purposes. If he lists his choices as Welsh history at Aberystwyth, geography at Aberdeen, engineering at Cambridge, biology at London, law at Kent and philosophy at Oxford, he is not likely to be taken very seriously. He should be clear about the subject he wishes to study, and should supply himself with the prospectuses of the universities recognised as excelling in that subject and go through them with care. Above all, he should take the advice of the head of his school on where he stands the best chance of success.

Once admitted, he has then to decide in detail the courses he proposes to take. A good university will take great pains to channel him through his university days in the paths best suited to his aims and abilities. As often as not he will be urged not to be too precipitate in his decisions. The tendency is towards a general first year in which the rudiments of the academic approach are taught, with increasing specialisation coming in the second and third years. It is not at all uncommon for a student, after getting his first glimpse into the astounding variety offered by a university, to rethink his purposes and opportunities and to branch off in a direction quite different from that leading to his original goal, provided, of course, that he can persuade his teachers he will do better in his new field.

Assuming he achieves a high quality junior degree he may, if his teachers are willing to recommend him, stay on for a further year to take a higher degree. This involves him in still closer specialisation and intensive study, very often in research work, and more intimate collaboration with his teachers. Finally, he may seek a research scholarship or fellowship, or work under supervision for a doctorate, for which he will probably have to write a thesis illuminating whatever field of research he has decided to enter. Normally he will spend all his undergraduate years in the same university, though he may spend some terms at a foreign university, especially if studies would benefit from it, i.e. if he is taking a degree in the language and literature, history or sociology of some region. For his higher degree or doctorate, however, he may well transfer to a different university where the specialisms are orientated more in his direction.

The student body is therefore split into undergraduates who have not yet taken their first degree, graduates who are studying for a higher degree and research students and others preparing for a doctorate or working on special research projects if they have already attained one.

The academic staff has a hierarchy of its own. At the top is the chancellor, normally an honorary position granted as a mark of distinction to a leading personality. He is appointed in the manner set out in the statutes, usually by the court or the council or by both acting in association. He will probably preside on major academic occasions, and may be consulted on important policy decisions, but he rarely, if ever, exercises personal executive power. He is the university's constitutional monarch. The executive head is the vice-chancellor. He also is appointed by the university as a whole operating through its statutory organs, and usually holds office until retirement or resignation. He will preside over the senate, or over higher bodies in the absence of the chancellor, and the main business of the university will be carried out over his signature. He is usually entitled to act on his own authority in an emergency, and since universities are prone to emergencies this is no light responsibility. He is assisted by a treasurer or finance officer who deals with the university's finance, a registrar or secretary who is responsible for its material administration and a librarian. Next in line come the deans of the faculties or schools of study, then the professors each responsible for the direction of studies in his own subject; and finally the readers, senior lecturers, lecturers and assistant lecturers who together make up the main body of the academic staff. The overall proportion of staff to students throughout the British university system was about 1–11 in the academic year 1969–70. When one adds together the dons and the administrative staff, which includes the library staff, laboratory technicians and demonstrators and the clerical and domestic help, the total comes to something like half the number of students. In a large university this makes up a very substantial body of souls, and the business of holding them together and maintaining the sense of direction of the institution as a whole must be one of the most delicate and sophisticated tasks human beings can be called upon to undertake. Vice-chancellors are a very special breed.

Indeed, control and administration lie at the root of most university problems. Throughout the remainder of this book, whether we are looking at dons or at students, we shall continually be driven back to questions of administration. In this chapter it has only been possible to give the briefest outline, to illustrate the skeleton of the organisation of learning. In what follows we shall be clothing it, like Ezekiel's bones in the desert, with flesh and sinew, blood and, I hope, the breath of life.

There is, however, one other general matter of organisation on which we have not yet touched which, because it lies outside the modern stream, is more suitably dealt with as an appendix or footnote to what has gone before—the special position occupied by Oxford and Cambridge. It is not just that they are ancient foundations or that they have developed an academic and social tradition that causes them to be ranked in a class of their own. From the point of view of organisation they are based on a college system which, though copied after a fashion elsewhere, is still unique of its kind. Both grew up as federations of colleges, each one founded independently and provided with its own sources of finance. This system is still maintained. Members of the university are first and foremost members of a college with its own rules and financial structure. There is a university syllabus and there are university examinations, but the life of the university is collegiate rather than monolithic. The freshman undergraduate is immediately submerged in college life, and his loyalties throughout his stay are first to his college and only second to the university. His most immediate teachers and advisers are usually Fellows of his own college, and although he may attend university lectures and enter into many purely university social and sporting activities, he remains throughout his life a Christchurch or Clare man (or a Girton or Somerville woman). It is this that gives these two universities their unique flavour.

Other ancient foundations also started out with a collegiate structure, primarily St Andrews, Aberdeen and Durham, but they no longer maintain it to the same degree. The most akin to Oxford and Cambridge is Durham, which is still largely collegiate in form, but the college functions there seem to be more domestic than academic in operation, and lack the Oxbridge flavour. The civic universities tended to take monolithic form from the beginning, with the possible exception of London, but that is a special case. It is more an amalgam of specialised institutions than a federation of colleges. Both University College and King's College could reasonably claim to be a university in their own right. People are apt to say 'I was at University College (or the LSE or Imperial College)' rather than 'I was at London', but that is more because they are effectively separate institutions than because of any organic feeling for them. The University of London can be compared, in this sense, with the University of Wales with its five separate colleges at Cardiff, Swansea, Aberystwyth, Bangor and Lampeter, each of which is intended as an individual university in its own right.

Three of the new universities—York, Lancaster and Kent—have adopted college organisation, but the exigencies of UGC financial control and the modern managerial methods of architecture and administration make it impossible for them to develop along Oxbridge lines. They have not enjoyed the spacious elbow room offered by individual founders and a more leisured age. Kent, possibly, most closely approaches the Oxbridge ideal but all three, in spite of highly imaginative planning, seem to have more in common with the students' residences and student blocks one finds elsewhere. Nevertheless, it is noticeable that these three universities have suffered least from the student difficulties currently rife among their contemporaries. Decentralisation has its advantages. 'We are able to provide a job for every militant' is how one don described it to me, though I doubt if he really meant that a deliberate policy of *divide et impera* had been adopted. It is simply that smaller units of organisation tend to create closer personal contact between the different levels of the academic hierarchy.

As I have tried to make plain in this chapter, university organisation is very largely a problem of establishing a unity of interest and endeavour among a motley collection of highly idiosyncratic individuals. That calls for what in modern times is known as effective channels of communication. The more fluid and flexible the channels, the easier it is for the community to find stability and strength. The higher the degree of centralisation, however handy it may prove for computerisation, the more difficult it is to find room for the quirks and quiddities of individual needs. The college system may be archaic, but it has proved itself in as difficult social times as those we are passing through now. There is a lesson here for vice-chancellors everywhere.

No two universities are alike, and an attempt to describe them all would make dull reference-book reading. But it might be helpful to describe a single, mythical but typical university in a fair degree of detail. Neither the ancient foundations nor the new universities are typical, so let us imagine a civic university that has been expanded in the post-war period, reflecting both early tradition and modern trends. We shall call it the University of Bolderdale, a regional description tradition-ally used to describe three adjacent counties, similar to East Anglia or Galloway. We shall have occasion to refer to it frequently in most of the chapters that follow.

The history of the University of Bolderdale is typical of the period. The vigorous and ancient port of Morendon, an industrial city of growing importance, had established a technical school in the 1880s. From the turn of the century it had petitioned regularly for a charter that would transform this small beginning into a full-blown university, but had met with resistance from successive governments until, in 1924, through one of the more memorable acts of the first Labour admini-stration, a charter suddenly appeared. The land had long since been deeded by a local magnate, and the good citizens of Morendon had been building up a fund to meet the initial costs. In 1925 the first of the new buildings began to rise. It was constructed of local stone and was dignified with a fine central dome, a miniature of St Paul's, with long, broad corridors reaching out to east and west to provide offices for the professors and lecturers. A fine library, capable of housing 200,000 volumes, was built nearby, and in subsequent years other less magnifi-cent buildings were clustered round the central core. By 1935 there were over 1,000 students, mostly drawn from the locality, though among them an increasing number of outsiders. It was in the early 1950s, when the student body had risen to 1,700, that the government decided Bolderdale was fit for expansion and dangled before the present Vice-Chancellor's predecessor the prospect of massive grants of funds, provided of course through the then still moderately prophylactic screen of the University Grants Committee. The Vice-Chancellor was too good an academic not to sense the danger, but too shrewd a businessman not to take advantage of the offer. He succeeded in making a deal on the general basis that the university would decide on the lines of academic expansion but the government should have the last word in material provision. The contractors moved in early in 1953 and the stately, if inefficient, core of Bolderdale was cocooned, first in a sea of mud, then in a growing web of concrete and glass. The government was more lavish in those days than it was later forced to become, and the old Vice-Chancellor knew how to make the best of his opportunities. The physics building might not rival the Parthenon, but it has an air of grandeur and permanence, even though the action of wind and weather on its shoddy materials have already given it a somewhat Dorian Gray appearance. The new arts building on the far side is rather utilitarian by comparison, but it is much superior to the rabbit hutches and bathing compartments that distinguish many of the buildings of the 1960s crop of universities. When he was succeeded in 1958 by Sir Piers MacHine, the foundations of the School of Environment were being laid, its professors and Dean had been appointed and their general terms of reference had been settled. Sir Piers's inheritance was closely defined, but like most of his northern compatriots he was capable of moulding it, and equally of conjuring additional funds both out of the Treasury and out of the pockets of the people of Bolderdale. Today Bolderdale has nearly 5,500 students, an academic staff of over 500, and a reputation that has stirred many an older foundation to envy if not to successful emulation.

Bolderdale's form of government stems from its origins. It has a Court which normally meets once a year, which is as representative of the Bolderdale establishment as it is of the academic body and which exercises about as much effective authority as the Consultative Assembly of the Council of Europe—that is to say, it enunciates principles that may or may not be adhered to, according to the compulsive pressures of the moment. Its Chairman is the Chancellor, Lord Switherwell, the only Bolderdale *alumnus* to have achieved Cabinet rank, and its membership is made up of the university's principal executive officers, deans of faculties and schools, departmental heads, representatives of the general teaching body and, more recently, of the students. Its lay members, who outnumber the dons, include the chairmen of the main trusts that contribute to the funds (though their contribution, which was once dominant, now represents a miniscule contribution to total cost), the Lords Lieutenants of the three counties of Bolderdale, representatives of the county councils, of the Morendon Urban Council, of half a dozen leaders of religious communities, the President of the Morendon Chamber of Commerce, the Chairman of the Morendon Port Authority and the Chief Constable of Bucknelshire in which county Morendon is located. This last member, who has become the chief target of student disapproval, owes his appointment to the fact that the Privy Councillors nominated by the 1924 Labour Party to advise on the charter were not particularly skilled in the use of the Royal Prerogative and extremely suspicious of the civil servants whose duty it was to advise them. The then Chief Constable had, in a personal capacity, played a large part in presenting the petition, and the Privy Councillors insisted on nominating him by office rather than in person, believing with characteristic socialist zeal that public office was of much greater importance than private quality. The total membership of the Court is 107. The average attendance at the annual meeting is 43.

Real power rests with the Council, which is composed of the leading academics and administrators, representatives of the teaching body and a token membership of the student body. It has a finger in every academic pie, and exercises ultimate authority on everything from admission to expulsion of students, from appointment to dismissal of staff, from the promulgation of regulations to their interpretation. Theoretically it is subject to the Court; in practice it has its own way.

Much of its work is done by the Academic Senate, presided over by the Vice-Chancellor and composed almost entirely of senior academics and representatives of the teaching body. There are no student representatives on the Academic Senate, but there soon will be if present trends continue. Still more detailed work is done by the Boards of Studies of the faculties and schools, and beneath them lie the departmental committees, on which students *are* represented.

Readers may well think that in terms of modern managerial theory this is a cumbrous method of decision-making. They would be quite right, but of such is the kingdom of the British academic community.

Then, of course, there is student organisation. This is simple, theoretically democratic and practically managerial. All students must be members of the union and must contribute £15 a year to it (which is actually included in their grants). There are no means of contracting out. A student who fails to pay his or her union dues is classed as being in debt to the university, and any student in debt to the university at the time of degree awards will not be awarded a degree. Thus there is strong compulsion to pay up. They receive many benefits. The union runs the refectory, organises and pays for all non-academic activities from the drama society to the football team, and through its affiliation to the National Union of Students offers its members cheap travel facilities as well as opportunities to participate in both academic and national politics. It organises student representation on such organs of university government as have places for them, and decides whether it will use a proportion of its ample funds for supporting political propaganda. Union meetings are only rarely attended by more than 25 per cent of the student body. Less than 2 per cent actually participate, even by remote democratic control, in its detailed work. We shall come back to this odd phenomenon when we deal with students and student/don relationships.

On the academic side, Bolderdale is noted for three particular excellencies: environmental studies with particular reference to urban development and transport problems, theoretical physics and applied science. Outside these fields it is much respected for its departments of English, politics and mathematics. In most other branches of learning it is competent. There is a Faculty of Arts and Social Sciences, a School of Environmental Studies, a Faculty of Natural Sciences and a Faculty of Applied Science. The Deans of these four divisions are, constitutionally speaking, the next most important figures in the university after the Vice-Chancellor. Each is a professor, and often a departmental head as well, usually of the department acknowledged to be the most important in that faculty or school. He is, saving the Vice-Chancellor, the ultimate authority on the admission of students; as Chairman of the Board of Studies he is pretty certain to get his own way in the long run. Universities are run by committees, and the don who rises high in the administrative hierarchy is the one who has learned how to run the committees that run the university.

The Faculty of Arts and Social Sciences includes departments of English, economics, sociology, philosophy, mathematics, psychology, history, politics, religion, linguistics and the history and philosophy of science. Neither classics nor modern languages is taught, though there is a language laboratory at which students can learn enough of any foreign language with which they need a nodding acquaintance to pursue certain aspects of their own studies. Ancient languages are considered irrelevant, and modern languages a skill rather than a subject for study in depth. Honours degrees are offered in English, economics, mathematics, psychology, politics, history and religious studies. The departments of sociology, philosophy, linguistics and the history and philosophy of science are service departments, providing ancillary courses. There is also a general degree for which the student must pass in courses offered by any three departments. An M.A. can be achieved by a fourth year's intensive work in any of the Honours subjects. Doctorates are also awarded, especially in English, politics and mathematics.

The School of Environmental Studies is one of the experimental creations of the post-war period. Its purpose is to study man's environment in relation to his life as a member of society, and although it has departments of its own it draws heavily on the other faculties (all of which are represented on its Board of Studies) for many of its courses. It has departments of geography, ecology, climatology, demography, transportation, urban development and town planning, agricultural history and comparative social organisation. It offers an Honours B.SC. after three years and an M.SC. after four. There is a wide variety of courses in which each of these can be obtained.

The Faculty of Natural Sciences covers B.SC.s physics, chemistry, botany, zoology, biology and geology, in all of which subjects Honours B.SC.s are offered. Its crowning joy, however, is its Department of Theoretical Physics on which much wealth has been lavished, and which is generally recognised as one of the best in the country. Its staff includes two Nobel prize-winners. Its D.PHIL. is highly prized, and its research work enjoys worldwide renown.

The Faculty of Applied Sciences specialises in various types of engineering and electronics, including a post-graduate research unit into medical engineering, i.e. the application of electronics to various medical and surgical devices, which works in close association with the town hospital. Its departments of transport engineering and pollution control provide courses for the School of Environmental Studies, as well as offering B.SC.s of their own. Its departments of electrical engineering and cybernetics both offer an Honours degree.

Bolderdale is certainly not the very best of universities and suffers from many gaps in its curriculum, but it is a good university in the sense that its range of studies is wide, and its staff carefully chosen and on the whole both competent and sincere. A Bolderdale degree can hold its own with the degrees of most of the older civic universities. Physicists and transport engineers from Bolderdale are welcome everywhere from Tokyo to Capetown. Of its 5,500 students, more than half come from the Bolderdale counties. Its main problem, like that of all state-supported universities, is finance. Raids on its endowments have left it with a private income of under £250,000 and most of its springs of new benefaction have dried up under the hot rays of estate duty and corporation tax. An appeal in the late 1960s for a new building for the students' union raised only a third of what was needed. The failure was put down to the outbursts of student disorder proliferating at that time, which was probably true but singularly unfair since its own troubles were muted compared to what happened elsewhere. Its main difficulties, therefore, flow from reliance on the government purse and from the increasing number of directives that come down to it. It is under severe pressure to continue enlarging itself, but the funds offered involve a constant trimming of the little extras that help to oil the wheels of academic life, extra research facilities for the staff, extra social facilities for students. Remittance men have little ambition and are usually able to rub along, but a good university is ambitious to excel, and it is hard for it to have to live under remittance man conditions. Like most universities, however, Bolderdale is fortunate in enjoying the support and loyalty of many dedicated dons, who struggle hard to make the best of things and are surprisingly successful, even in this age when values seem to be moulded more by cost benefit analysis than by the philosopher and the saint.

CHAPTER SIX

The academic profession

The academic profession probably enjoys fewer direct financial rewards than any other with the exception of the Church. No doubt many members of other professions would dispute this, all of us believing as we do that we are hardly done by in comparison to others, but the facts speak for themselves. Certainly schoolteachers are less well paid, but they do not need to be so highly qualified, and anyway their case merely reinforces the general argument that teaching, whether in school or higher education, is not one of the highways to great wealth. The senior academics who transmit their knowledge and techniques to the leaders of other professions earn far less than they do. There have indeed been cases of dons who have been able to buy themselves islands in the Caribbean, but that was due not to their academic salaries but to their ability to write essential textbooks that became a must for the students of all five continents. A very senior professor in a British university will now, after a long period of inflation, get as much as £7,000 a year. That is very low compared to a top medical consultant, the head of a firm of architects or the managing director of Omnium Limited, all positions that many dons could fill if they wished, and that some dons very occasionally do.

It has always been the same; more usually it has been very much worse. In 1910 a professor was paid £600 a year. True, he enjoyed many college privileges, plenty of free wine and comfortable rooms, but these were monastic blessings not to be shared with his wife and children in north Oxford. During the last sixty years the academic profession has risen faster on the economic scale than other professions, but it still has a long way to go before it catches them up. The question arises as to why there is still no lack of recruits to the academic community, especially in an age when money is so important that it has a literature of its own and not even the most moronic newspaper can hope to survive without at least a City Page. Why in such a world do so many highly intelligent people opt for the ill-paid academic life? With the Church it is a matter of faith, but the academic, even many a modern theologian, lacks the bouyancy offered by certainty in the matter of ultimate values, and is liable to sink without trace if he plots the wrong course. There must be some splendours in academic life to balance its financial miseries.

To anyone who has a bent for teaching and a sense of dedication to the pursuit of truth it offers a milieu free from many of the pressures of the world, so that both these activities can be practised under a fairly stout umbrella of security. One does not need to be a Nobel prizewinner or even a professor to be able to extract a profound sense of satisfaction from academic life. It can be a leisurely life compared to the routine of office, consulting room or factory; provided one does one's work well, one is largely one's own master, though here one must enter the *caveat* that the absence of the discipline of office hours can lead to a far heavier load of work, especially for those who look on work more as a way of life than as a means of paying for it. The social life has an intellectual content and breadth of interest that should satisfy all but the most exacting. There are many other satisfactions: that of drawing out bright young minds and of watching their subsequent progress through life; the pleasure of throwing fresh light on a problem still unsolved; the joy of occupying some temporarily impregnable salient across the frontier of knowledge; and, in later years, the enjoyment of looking back over a life rich in personalities and contacts with some of the most profound minds of the age. These are quiet achievements, but none the less satisfying. Then there are the rewards of status—the occupation of a Chair, maybe, or the Wardenship of an Oxbridge college, the control of a department or a faculty or the succession to a vice-chancellorship, or the award of an honorary degree by some other university as a mark of professional respect. For those who like travel there are opportunities to teach and to study abroad; for those who like leisure—fewer people than one might suppose—there are many vacations. But the real appeal of the academic life is its proximity to the frontier, the opportunities it offers for intellectual adventure. To this it owes the *élan vital* that has inspired it since the days of Plato's Academy—the urge to explore, to discover, to master the unknown; the same drive that took Marco Polo into China, Columbus to the New World, and da Gama to India, Mungo Park to the Niger and Livingstone to the heart of Africa. I almost added 'and St Paul to Rome', but he was driven by certainty, the others by inquiry, by doubt. The call of the academic life is heard and responded to by every pioneer.

Equally the academic life has its pains and penalties, like every other frontier activity. There are few Bentleys or Cadillacs on the campus, and the one or two parked there probably belong to student militants. There are dons in the best clubs, but rarely in the best restaurants. Leading couturiers do not establish salons in university towns. That, however, is the least of academic troubles, and comparatively few dons take it to heart, although the recently established Association of University Teachers (AUT), at which we shall take a brief look in the next chapter, has, very reasonably since it is a trade union, taken the matter up.

The principal misery of academic life is endemic, not external. A community is more difficult to live in than the world at large. It is small, circumscribed and, in spite of its breadth of interest, narrow and parochial in its domestic attitudes. Everything is near at hand, nothing is remote. In a university one continually rubs shoulders with one's colleagues, far more frequently than in any other profession. It has a life of its own with which everyone must be identified. There is no escape from it. We shall consider some of the results of this in Chapter Eight; for the moment it is sufficient to say that the academic profession is no place for the man or woman who cannot stomach pettiness and intrigue, jealousy and malice, disloyalty and betrayal. Those who succeed are those who rise above that kind of pond life. They are in a majority, but the sediment is substantial, endlessly troublesome and often very sad.

Other academic miseries spring directly from the world itself. One can spend years on research in a particular field only to find oneself pre-empted on the point of success by a colleague in a neighbouring university or a different country who has been approaching the problem from another and more fruitful direction. One can strive for a Chair, and see it awarded to a brilliant colleague junior to oneself. One can labour for a year on an article for a learned journal, and have it rejected as out of date. Such disappointments occur in other professions, but they are rarely the product of so wholehearted an outpouring of life-blood, nor so conclusive in their results. The by-passed academic has few other avenues of endeavour; he has to live with his failures to a degree that others need not. The failed stockbroker can move into merchant banking or industry, the retired serviceman into estate management or personnel work. The don who has not made a go of it is only rarely fitted for other occupations. He must go on living in the academic world. Some take to politics, but the best politicians are rarely former dons. This is perhaps the greatest drawback of the academic profession—there is little chance of escape from it.

Those who decide that the academic life has a balance of advantages over disadvantages and choose it as a career have an unusual motivation, remote from the urges that take most people into law, commerce, engineering or accountancy. Certainly there are those who choose it, mistakenly, as a soft option, but they are apt to come to the same grief that eventually overtakes the soft-option hunter in any walk of life. Some enter it because they have a vocation for teaching, especially for the kind of teaching that is needed after schooling has laid the foundations for higher study. They are eager for the opportunity of helping the developing mind to stretch itself and to master the techniques of learning and inquiry. The great dons of the past have also been the great teachers, able to excite curiosity, to explain clearly the principles of knowledge, to illustrate their interrelationship and to show how one moves stage by stage from what can easily be grasped to the more recondite theories and speculations that bring one up to the boundaries of research. Others enter the academic world because they are fascinated by learning for its own sake; they have tasted its pleasures in their own days as undergraduates and graduate students, and have become 'hooked'. The mere act of teaching helps to increase their own knowledge. It is one thing to do well in an examination and to impress one's examiners with what one has been able to absorb; to be able to transmit that knowledge to the immature mind one must understand it in greater depth.

From the moment of taking up his first university post the young don has to persevere in his own learning. It is one of the cardinal principles of university organisation that he must be allowed time to do so. Nowadays, when every human activity is measured quantitively in terms of productivity and visible results, outsiders are apt to look askance at the apparently short time a don actually spends in teaching. They forget the long hours needed to prepare a course of lectures—and to amend them after their first delivery has shown up their flaws and inadequacies. They forget, too, the imperative need to keep up to date in an age when the explosion of knowledge is proceeding in a geometrical progression; there is no less effective teacher than he who is not constantly improving his understanding of his subject, or he who forgets that anyone working constantly in terms of imponderables must enjoy periods for intellectual refreshment and speculation if he is not to become stale and pass his staleness on to those he is supposed to quicken and excite.

In 1969 the UGC, driven by its masters' demands for economies, circulated to a large number of dons a questionnaire on the amount of time each devoted to various activities. It was not very well received. There was no difficulty in giving precise figures for lectures, tutorials and seminars, for reading or for specific research, but time for thought and speculation is another matter. I know of one young mathematics don who enjoyed a sudden insight in the middle of the morning coffee break and rushed straight back to his room to get it down on paper. The result was a new mathematical theorem of considerable value, which incidentally helped to earn him a Chair at an unusually early age. It is difficult to see how he could have fitted that bit of creative work into the questionnaire. Perhaps the most compelling attraction of university life is that the dedicated learner is not only offered paid time for learning, but is actually expected to engage in it as a duty.

This love of learning is the main drive that provides the universities with dons, but they have other qualities—detachment from material success in the commercial sense, vocation and dedication, objectivity, perhaps serenity or something closely approaching it. By no means all dons possess all these attributes. The academic profession is as uneven in excellence as any other, an unevenness caused as much by the pressures which the profession itself and the conditions inherent in its practice impose as by the quirks and failures of individuals. There is, for instance, 'donnishness'.

'Donnish' is one of these Humpty-Dumpty words that means exactly what its user wants it to mean. It can be pejorative in one mouth, a form of compliment in another. On the whole, however, it carries an implication of something too wide of the norm to be wholly acceptable, something moreover that is not at all attractive. Some years ago *Punch* carried a donnish joke. The cartoon showed two gowned figures looking at a blackboard covered by some fifteen lines of mathematical symbols ending up with '. . . $= x^{-2}$'. 'Very witty,' says one to the other. Dons do tend to look on themselves as members of a very superior group, and to put a special value on the gift of one-upmanship. In this they differ from members of other professions—or, to put it another way, when members of other professions show themselves to have similar tendencies they are accused of being donnish. There is a flavour of secrecy about it, of an inner circle, of particularity, of concerns superior to the day-to-day business of lesser beings. We are all personally involved in contracts and leases, medical care, road-building and sewers, balance sheets and income tax returns; very, very few of us are immediately affected by the niceties of Middle English grammar, the methodology of Descartes or the finer points of nuclear physics. But donnishness is not just a matter of distinction between don and layman. It also carries a purely domestic implication of superiority between don and don. Senior Common Room conversation is in the nature of a display of expertise, a tennis match in which style and elegance are as important as speed or spin. Donnishness calls for an audience.

Verbal dexterity is a necessary component of donnishness. A well-turned sentence, brief, pointed and probably containing a veiled reference to some pertinent esoterica that the listener ought to know but probably does not, is the kind of backhand that comes spinning across the net. If it can be returned by an obscure quotation that shows close acquaintance with the esoterica, the opponent notches up a point. The listener can almost detect a triumphant mutter of 'deuce'. Long practice produces a suavity that makes the whole process a delight to the observer, though younger dons are often no more than brash, abrasive and irritating, and a good many older dons can be even worse if they have not mellowed enough to bring charm to the game. The legendary Jowett, Master of Balliol, seems, from one source at any rate, to provide a case in point. In *Fifty-Five Years at Oxford*[1], George Beardoe Grundy describes how, as a very young academic, he was walking along Parks Road with a senior Fellow of his college when they saw Jowett walking towards them on the opposite pavement. 'Ah, there is the Master,' said the senior Fellow, 'let us cross and speak with him.' They did so, and as they came together the senior Fellow exclaimed: 'Master, I have just been reading the splendid translation you have just published. May I send you a few comments on it?' 'Pray don't,' Jowett replied and passed on.

The idea of donnishness did not of course originate in the academic world. It is a layman's term, a reaction against the abrasive effect on the lay mind of the don at large. Outside his academic milieu, the don can seem pedagogic and pedantic, assuming the authority of a teacher and insisting on fine points of meaning that are normally overlooked. He gives an impression of 'effortless superiority', not because he believes he really enjoys it but because his whole life is devoted to bringing people up to his own level, which induces habits of speech and behaviour that are out of place in wider surroundings.

And yet dons are really no different from other people. One can paraphrase Shylock: 'Does not a don live? Does he not hunger? Does he not bleed?' In the matter of physical appearance dons are exactly the same as everybody else. There are philosophy dons who look like family solicitors, chemists who would pass in a crowd for grocers, biologists who might be stockbrokers, historians who might have come straight from a desk at the Inland Revenue. In the same way, there are doctors who make one think of poets, poets who look like navvies, and navvies who look like doctors. Dons have the virtues and failings as well as the appearance of the rest of humankind. 'We have some very energetic young Fellows nowadays,' sighed Maurice Bowra when questioned by the Press about Bill Deakin, who had parachuted into enemy-occupied Yugoslavia during the second world war—a donnish remark if ever there was one.

When it comes to the defence of liberty, one can count on the academic community standing in the front line, and every pettiness can be matched by a generosity, for that is the life-blood of any community. Apparent conceit is perhaps no more than a reaction against an ingrained humility

[1] Methuen, London, 1945.

imposed by having to live with the awful realisation of ignorance, a realisation that most dons but few laymen share. The don is essentially humane. He knows too much about the frailty of human nature to be otherwise. If I were to be judged and looked more for mercy than for my deserts, I would prefer it to be by a jury of dons than one of housewives or politicians or certain churchmen.

All that is generalisation. Let us look at some of the people in the University of Bolderdale. Sir Piers MacHine, the Vice-Chancellor, graduated in law from London in the mid-1930s. He went into the Civil Service, and from there into business. In the second world war he held a senior position on the army staff, and was afterwards appointed to the Board of one of the New Town Corporations. Towards the end of the 1950s he was appointed Vice-Chancellor of Bolderdale. Already in his early sixties, he will probably be retiring in the course of a year or two. He has great executive ability and a flair for understanding people and getting on with them. Though not a professional academic himself, he has a thorough understanding of the nature and purpose of university life. He is good at delegation, but takes pains to keep himself fully informed of all that is going on in his bailiwick. He cannot know all his students personally but he makes sure that they know him and that he is always accessible to those who wish to see him. But he does know all his academic staff, though he rarely intervenes decisively in any but the most senior appointments. He has a gift for detecting signs of any major upheaval in advance, and if he cannot always nip it in the bud he has the tact and tenacity to ride out the storm. He is not particularly popular, but he is respected and on the whole deferred to. An attempt was made to unseat him at a time when the university was in the worst throes of its second expansion period, but it failed. Since then there have been occasional cabals against him, none of them successful, not even a majority of the sociology staff lined up with a group of militant students to resist an appointment in the Department of Politics. He looks younger than his age, and has something of the bearing of an army divisional commander. Donnish is the last word to use of him; he is an efficient sophisticated machine, well oiled by a fluid sense of humour and sufficiently flexible to be able to cope with dons and students alike.

The Dean of the Faculty of Arts and Social Sciences is Professor Pontifex Prime. He is also Head of the Department of Politics. He is a small, eager man in his early sixties who graduated from London, took a D.Phil. at Oxford and eventually became Professor of Government at one of the civic universities in the Midlands. Sir Piers MacHine's predecessor brought him to Bolderdale to set up the new Department of Politics in 1952. His reputation as a vivid reliable lecturer able to excite the interest of his students was then only beginning to grow; it was a far-sighted recommendation from Oxford that won him the job. Professor Prime has a brisk, almost abrupt manner. Though he cannot stomach the lazy or the stupid, he will take infinite pains with any student who shows the faintest signs of promise. He lectures with gusto, and sets out from the first to command the imagination and curiosity of his listeners, while in his tutorials he is capable of sympathy and severity in equal abundance.

He was elected Dean some five years ago, and was re-elected after his first term of three years in spite of the vociferous opposition of the sociologists, who feel he fails to take their self-imposed political mission as seriously as they take it themselves. He is married, but he and his wife live on the campus as sole occupants of one of the original group of twelve professors' houses put up by an early benefactor, most of which have now been sub-divided, and is available to students and staff colleagues at all hours. It is said openly by the left-wingers that he shows a deplorable degree of right-wing bias, but right-wing dons and students complain bitterly of the reverse. As Dean, he has a big say in admissions policy and is responsible for discipline. His severity certainly comes out in both capacities. His opening question to applicants for his own department—'Do you want to study politics for intellectual or vocational reasons?'—is followed by a probing cross-examination if the interviewee admits to political ambitions; but he never turns down anyone, however far to right or left, who can show a fair measure of intellectual backing for his views and a genuine desire to study. In matters of discipline he is intolerant of organised upheavals but too skilled in the practice of his own subject to show it overtly. We shall hear more about him.

On the whole, Pontifex Prime could be described as belonging to the old school of dons. Representative of the brave new academic world is Professor George Browne, who is Head of the Department of Sociology. He is young as professors go, having been still in his first year at Morendon Grammar School in 1940. After his military service, in the course of which, due to circumstances entirely within his own control, he failed to rise to commissioned rank, he won a first in politics at Manchester and took a PH.D. in social history at Leeds. He has a genius for picking soft options, and a quick eye for personal advantage. The emergent discipline of sociology, with its hazy boundaries and growing popularity, seemed to offer a growth area that could be both enjoyable and profitable. By 1953 he was a lecturer, by 1960 a senior lecturer. In 1963 he gravitated to Essex, but early in 1965 Bolderdale advertised for a professor to plan and guide a new department of sociology with special emphasis on its environmental connotations. Mr George Browne had worked hard and had a more than nodding acquaintance with most of the fields in which sociology grazed. He applied. His old headmaster at Morendon Grammar School happened to be a lay member of the University Court. In 1965, Professor George Browne took up his new duties at the age of 39, bringing with him, as wife, a serious, bespectacled young woman whom he had guided to a First at Essex. The Professor is good-looking, intelligent, extrovert and eager for the applause of his juniors. He appears a great deal on television, especially Independent Television which pays better. He has surrounded himself with a staff of younger men, intelligent, extrovert and equally eager for the applause of their juniors. The Bolderdale Department of Sociology enjoys high prestige in the sociological world, and receives annually four times as many applications for admission as it can accept. If candidates for admission had been voters, Professor Browne would have been Dean of the Faculty instead of Professor Prime.

The sociology undergraduates and a fair number of junior sociology dons have been at the root of such disturbances as Bolderdale has suffered in the last five years. They argue, not unreasonably, that since society is their study they have a right to speak on social questions. Mrs Browne has produced no babies, but she has written three articles for learned journals published by the Pergamon Press, and has given two esoteric talks on Radio 3. The couple live in a flat above a pub in the Morendon Docks, which they have decorated on principles indicated in the *Observer* colour supplement. Students are welcome on Tuesday and Thursday evenings. It is a notorious centre of university politics.

Possibly the most popular don at Bolderdale is Dr P. S. Yardley, the Reader in Anthropology. He is popular among the dons because he keeps himself well outside all cliques and cabals, is courteous and friendly and a complete stranger to the malice that flourishes in university soil. He is popular with the students for he has a genuine love of the young and is invariably accessible. He has a sympathetic gift for understanding personal problems and for communicating good advice without any hint of superiority or patronage. He is also a born teacher. There is no anthropology degree at Bolderdale, but his lectures are well attended. He has published no great learned work, but his three collections of essays sell regularly in the university bookshop and further afield as well; there are few bookshops in university cities where they are not kept in stock. A bachelor nearing retiring age, he is the very picture of a stage don with a fuzz of hair round the back of a domed bald head and unruly *pince-nez*. He is called 'Yardley' by dons and students alike; only the very old Bolderdale hands and the registry clerks could tell you what the 'P.S.'

stand for. He lives on the ground floor of one of the former professors' houses, in a flat littered with books which he lends to students with a rash prodigality that is matched by the regularity with which they are returned. There is, alas, much pilfering from the university bookshop, but it is a tradition amounting to a point of student honour that Yardley's books must go back where they belong.

Of the three professors' houses that have not suffered conversion, one is occupied by Professor Prime and the other two by Professor Harry Nucleus, Head of the Department of Theoretical Physics, and Professor David Crane, the authority on dock transport and engineering. Professor Nucleus is a Nobel prizewinner, an eminent researcher and also a gifted teacher. Apart from a few general lectures each term he works mainly with post-graduates, each of whom he personally selects. However, he knows every one of his undergraduates, follows their development with jealous care and from them builds up the research teams that have made his department world-famous. He is a tall, heavily-built, pouchy-eyed and pouchy-clothed man with a surgeon's hands and the stamina of a horse. He is also President of the Bolderdale Music Society, and devotes much of his spare time to its affairs.

Professor Crane, by contrast, is a small, brisk, military man, and did in fact come to prominence during the war as one of the designers and executants of the Mulberry Harbour that made D-Day possible. Like Professor Browne, he is a Morendon man, but is the product of a state school. He joined the army as a boy, and was eventually carried up to the rank of brigadier by a talent for improvisation, ingrained engineering skill and the high casualty rates in Docks Maintenance Units. After leaving the army he was employed by the Morendon Dock Authority until Sir Piers tempted him into the university. He is a strict disciplinarian (he was sergeant-major of a sapper company for two years) and militants in his department are either quickly subdued or quickly got rid of. He has been the target of two unsuccessful demonstrations.

Most of the converted flats are occupied by bachelor junior dons or by young husband and wife teams. There is, for instance, Dr Evelyn Ballad, still in her twenties, disturbingly beautiful and distressingly remote, who is a specialist in the seventeenth-century minor poets and also lectures on the drama of that period. She is much in demand with the Bolderdale Dramatic Society and played Mrs Frail in their recent production of *Love for Love*. Then there is Angus MacIntyre, a tall, raw-boned Scot from Aberdeen, who lectures on moral philosophy and is one of the innumerable dons in innumerable universities who are writing books on the Nichomachaen Ethics of Aristotle. And Gordon and Mabel Prickett, both micro-biologists and both desperately earnest.

They hold coffee evenings for freshmen which tend to become less well attended as the autumn term draws to a close.

Another of the flats is occupied by the university chaplain. Bolderdale was originally a Congregational foundation, but that aspect of its community life began to fade as government money moved in. The chapel is now interdenominational, and is shared by Roman Catholics, Anglicans and Free Churchmen. The chaplaincy is, however, well endowed, and the office continues. The present incumbent is a young Welshman, the Rev. Joel Jones, small, dark, enthusiastic and an immense worker. He lectures on the philosophy of religion and runs the University Mission in the docks, in which he gets much help from sociology students. Professor Browne does not approve, but finding himself unable to do anything about it makes half-hearted and not very welcome efforts to insinuate himself into its management.

The vast majority of the dons live away from the campus, mostly in the Victorian and Edwardian villas that are the inner cocoon of Morendon. Very few have managed to get into the outer cocoon of council estates, but in 1960 the local council was prevailed on to grant the university planning permission for 30 acres to the north-west of the town, and there it built what has come to be known as University Village, containing homes for all grades of staff and employees as well as an area of flatlets for students, a community centre and a small market. Some forty of the dons live there, and the community has a flourishing social life which has done a great deal for staff/student relations. On the whole, the dons at University Village have a stronger sense of personal identity with the university than those in the town or in the neighbouring villages and countryside, though there are exceptions on both sides. They vary from young marrieds like the Wallaseys to old marrieds like the Rickerts. Frederick Wallasey lectures on economic history and Edna on biology. They have two small children who go to a private kindergarten run for the children of dons—and students nowadays—while Edna Wallasey is attending to her academic duties. Edward Rickerts is Reader in Bolderdale History and students are apt to find him something of a bore, but his wife, a homely woman in her early fifties, has appointed herself unpaid welfare officer to the Village and does more for the students there than most of the official 'counsellers' put together.

Another unusual couple are Sir Maurice and Lady Basingstoke. In 1965 Sir Maurice was a senior Treasury official, but in that year, discouraged perhaps by the odd behaviour of his political masters, he wrote privately to his old friend Sir Piers MacHine about a vacancy at Bolderdale for a Senior Lecturer in Public Administration in the Department of Politics. Normally some damage can be done to academic harmony if outsiders are brought in to occupy senior posts, but Sir Maurice had taken a double First in Modern Greats and had maintained his scholarly interests throughout his public service. Professor Prime jumped at the opportunity to bring in a scholar with such a wealth of practical experience, and in the spring of 1966 the Basingstokes moved into a Victorian villa in one of the better Morendon suburbs. Sir Maurice is a tall, slender man of great charm and courtesy. He is noted especially for the quality of his seminars on relations between officials and politicians, which are lively and well attended and which he guides with an intellectual power that wins the respect even of the militants. His occasional coffee evenings were not originally intended as a challenge to the George Brownes' hospitality, but became so all the same. The villa has a large garden which Mary Basingstoke, with the help of paid student labour, has restored to much of its original glory. Unlike most dons, Sir Maurice is a reasonably wealthy man—he comes from an old Bolderdale industrial family—and can afford such luxuries. During the summer term there are tennis parties that bring back a whiff of Edwardian days.

There is not much else at Bolderdale to recall the Oxbridge tradition. It is essentially a civic university with a heavy modern overlay. The staff club is exactly what it is called, a club rather than a Senior Common Room. It has a good, well-patronised bar—though not as large as that in Sheffield which boasts what I am sure is the longest academic bar in the country—an imaginative snack bar, a restaurant and a vast lounge, furnished with cheap but comfortable chairs and couches, which is packed at morning coffee time, and for half an hour or so after lunch. It is less well patronised at teatime, when the dons are busy getting rid of the day's work in order to get back to their families and television sets. Dinner is confined to a few bachelors, grass widowers or late workers, a dreary affair in the partially-lit restaurant slapped down by two somewhat resentful waitresses eager to get home. There is more academic life in the Students' Union and the Community Centre in University Village —political meetings, dances, religious discussions, chess matches and an enormous amount of general conversation. Dons share in much of it.

What distinguishes Bolderdale from Oxbridge is that at Bolderdale dons mix comparatively little socially among themselves. As far as they do mix, they talk shop as businessmen do. At lunch or during morning coffee or at tea they draw into little groups. Departments, especially departments of English, have a habit of making a large circle in one corner of the lounge and discussing—well, English I suppose—across an array of empty cups and ash-filled saucers. Members of academic committees discuss their tactics at the next meeting. Insurgent dons hold dark discussions about forthcoming student demos. It is all very much market-place stuff, a world apart from the high table of tradition where the circulating port encouraged speculation and dogmatism about the frontier, and a great deal of donnish bitchiness and donnish dirty stories on the side.

I am trying to point a difference, not to make what is nowadays called a value judgement. Bolderdale reflects the academic community of today, and if history is any guide, what is happening now is a great deal more important than what happened yesterday. The historical reasons for our being as we are today are important as aids to our understanding of ourselves, but the past does not set an example that the present should necessarily copy. That way lies stagnation, *pace* the nostalgia that settles on everyone over forty. The Bolderdale dons, just like the Bolderdale students, are the products of this electronic age. None the less, the Bolderdale academic community has its roots in the past. It is oriented in the direction of learning. Even Professor George Browne is struggling to disentomb the truth. Even the most troublesome militant is at Bolderdale because he wants to learn. All of them inherit, if not the tradition, at any rate the provenance of the past; they are its organic heirs, begotten not created. But like each successive generation they reflect the generation gap that is one of the most significant factors in today's society. As a group they still share in the qualities I listed at the beginning of the chapter, but they have adapted their methods to new circumstances. They are no less an academic community, no less dedicated, no less clannish; but many an Edwardian don would view them aghast—perhaps with a certain shocked envy, like our great grandmothers confronted by the mini-skirt. One would like to hear Jowett's comments, let alone those of Newman or Keble.

These changes are bound to have had their effect on the nature and quality of university life. It is therefore worth studying them in more detail, which we shall do in the next chapter. But it is not just the changing don that is important in this connection. The student has changed too, and we shall come to him—and her—at a later stage.

CHAPTER SEVEN

The changing don

Shortly after the second world war the Reform Club in London entered on the traumatic experience of adjusting to a social change that until then it had successfully ignored. At successive Annual General Meetings someone was sure to raise the question of the admission of women guests. At first the idea was laughingly put to one side, but battle was soon joined in earnest, and by the early 1950s it was agreed that they might be invited to dine in a secluded corner of the coffee room on Friday nights. For a year, it is said, the die-hards managed to maintain the proviso 'but no lavatory facilities',[1] but soon the necessary accommodation was offered, the exclusively male apparatus being modestly hidden by screens. Today ladies are admitted every week-night and even trouser suits, at first officially frowned on, are no longer uncommon. Oxford went through a similar, but more long-drawn-out experience in the second half of the nineteenth century until, in 1877, the statutes were altered to allow dons to marry instead of living in intermittent sin.

Permission to marry, however, was not the first concession to modernity. Earlier, Oxford had accepted the principle of the lay Fellow, a violent breach of the tradition that all Fellows had to be in holy orders. Marriage was the second, larger stone dislodged from the crumbling dam. It was followed by other stones in an avalanche that grew in volume as university power expanded at the expense of college power, but it was the simple right of the don to marry that was to have the most profound and far-reaching influence on the academic community. The change was slow in making itself felt, for the university was full of entrenched bachelors few of whom had any desire to change their condition. Gradually, however, the newer, younger dons began to grasp their opportunities. Each college still made its own restrictive rules—some insisted at first on celibate residence in term-time and permitted connubial bliss in vacations only— but it was a Canute-type resistance. The immediate beneficiaries, apart from the dons who took the plunge, were the landowners of

[1] In the neighbouring Travellers' Club, with its heavy Foreign Office membership, the opposition based itself on what was more diplomatically termed 'geographical difficulties'.

north Oxford, which quickly became a vast wilderness of Victorian villas.

Permissiveness breeds more thorough permissiveness. It is a gravitational process that begins slowly but gathers speed until, as we are learning today, it reaches the norm of thirty-two feet per second per second. The foundation of women's colleges followed rapidly and, as a natural consequence, women dons, initially quasi-dons—a far more notable innovation than women married to dons—began to invade the academic community. Tennyson lived to see the first burgeoning of *The Princess* from fantasy into fact. But as far as fundamental change is concerned it was the abandonment of academic celibacy that made the real difference. From that point of view, the introduction of women dons provided a conservative influence. They tended to be more celibate than the men.

Academic life was originally pure community life. The dons worked and lived together in a very close-knit web of association, with students equally closely integrated into groups. Celibacy is after all of the essence of community life. There have been attempts at mixed communities, particularly in the United States in the flowering days of New England, but they have rarely survived for long. Monasteries and nunneries have survived over the centuries, but even the Israeli kibbutzim find themselves in difficulties. Celibacy is an aid to concentration and single-mindedness; marriage may make a man or a woman more human, which is an advantage, but it also brings in its wake a whole crop of urgent and distracting problems, together with competing interests of a peculiarly delectable kind. The Roman Catholic clergy offer a unique advertisement in favour of compulsory celibacy, but outside the sphere of religion it is not a condition that can easily be imposed. When universities broke their religious ties, it ceased to be practicable. For the layman, celibacy can be very much of a stop-the-world-I-want-to-get-off attitude to life; marriage brings the world not just to the door but right into the bedroom. It is death to the idea of community living; it proved fatal to the old concept of a university as a closed community devoted to learning.

Not that that was a bad thing. Oxford and Cambridge were becoming sterile. For all its brilliance, the work of the tractarians of the nineteenth century was largely irrelevant to life, possibly even irrelevant to theology, which is nothing if not a life science. Unfortunately, once the pendulum starts to move there is no stopping it until it has reached the limit of its reverse swing. It looks as though that point has just about been reached, for the modern don would seem to be almost the precise opposite of the don of a hundred years ago. His relations with the university are no longer the close organic ties of complete commitment. He is doing a job, not living a way of life. He is centred on home and family, not on Hall, Chapel, Common Room and study. He may be just as conscientious, perhaps even more conscientious because he has his hostages to fortune to provide for, than his opposite number of the 1850s, but his horizons are limitless and he will be off after any other job that offers better prospects the minute his personal radar picks up a hint of it. In other words, the sense of local loyalty has diminished though the sense of professional duty may be just as strong or even stronger. Equally, student/teacher relationships have been changed. Certainly, there were plenty of dons in the old days who found students a nuisance and resented their disrupting influence on the college's monastic calm; but the mere fact of communal living fostered an essential solidarity between the two groups which is absent when only a few dons are residential and most of their colleagues hurry home as soon as the day's immediate work is done.

There is also the perennial question of making ends meet. The relatively low salaries paid to dons which we noted at the beginning of the last chapter are a hangover from the old tradition. It did not cost a bachelor don much to live in a well-endowed college, and his formal emoluments were correspondingly minimal. Scholarship became a traditionally low-paid profession, simply because the don received most of his reward in kind. Unlike the complete monastic, he had taken no vows of poverty and could be as fond of affluence as any other man. He might even be a man of substance in his own right, but even if he was poor he flourished within the community and benefited from its endowments— all those bottles of port and magnums of claret! (There was one splendid don—a proto-technologist—who invented a special table-railway for circulating the port more easily.) Today, as ordinary family breadwinners with wife and children to support, dons are no longer protected from the winds of economic change. Perhaps they write detective stories, a donnish occupation if every there was one. Perhaps they contrive television programmes. Perhaps they do some black-market outside tutoring, or take part in radio parlour games, operate as freelance journalists, give technical advice to Omnium Limited or even engage in business on their own account. The opportunities open to an intelligent and enterprising don are many and varied; his family should never starve. The trouble is that such opportunities are all too often remote from academic work and add significantly to the distractions arising out of normal family life.

Although I have been making a comparison between the dons of nineteenth-century Oxford and Cambridge and those of the Oxford and Cambridge of today, and although the communal lives of these ancient foundations have certainly suffered over the years, enough of the old atmosphere remains for them still to stand in startling contrast to the Bolderdales and new universities around them. The college system is still their predominant feature. If, however, one looks at the academic community as a whole the change is seen to be overwhelming. The modern don is a wage-earner, subject to precisely the same pressures as the members of other professions, vulnerable to the chill economic winds that play around the accountant, lawyer, sales manager, publisher or journalist. If anything, he is even more open to them on account of the salary basis the public purse inflicts on his calling. All the same, the effect of this sea change on the nature of the academic profession has been less total than might be supposed.[1]

In the first place, dons have not ceased to be donnish. That is a characteristic of the profession, little affected by externals. The good don—and there does not seem to have been any marked fall in the proportion of good dons (it may even have risen, for economic stress concentrates the mind just as effectively as the fear of being hanged tomorrow). The good don is still a frontiersman, loving learning for its own sake, apt to think in abstract terms, more inclined to sharpness of wit than robustness of humour and more capable of seeing beyond Plato's shadows on the wall than most people. Like the ministry, the academic profession colours the whole outlook of its members much more than does, say, medicine or engineering, though doctors tend to have a clinical approach to society and engineers are usually associated with hair-raising forms of enterprise.[2]

The good don remains a good teacher. If anything, he is a better teacher simply because he lives more in the world than his cloistered forerunner, just as the politician who earns money over and above his parliamentary salary is usually a better representative than the pure party hack, and as the best clergymen are usually those blessed with a sound working knowledge of sin. But here we must make two qualifications. The pressures of competition within the profession have put a premium on research which, if indulged in to excess, comes into collision

---

[1] Readers who would like more detailed information about dons than is given in these pages are advised to turn to *The British Academics* by Professors A. H. Halsey and Martin Trow (Faber & Faber, London, 1971). This highly specialised compilation and evaluation of statistical data on the academic life deals with such matters as the social origins of dons, their education, salaries, supplementary earnings, hopes for promotion, research activities, mobility from university to university, political views and affiliations, academic attitudes and so on. Practically the only aspect of dons it does not cover is their humanity, which is the special concern of the author of this work.

[2] The traditional army soubriquet awarded to the Royal Engineers, 'the mad sappers', is not without foundation.

with the exigencies of teaching. Formerly, a don had to be an enthusiast for research to engage in it to excess. Today it is becoming a career essential; opportunities of advancement are largely dependent on being able to show evidence of 'original work'. Applications for senior posts are weighed down by long lists of books written and articles published. While this may be the joy of the publishers of learned journals, and the despair of the librarians who have to find the money to buy them, it is also the source of a not altogether unfair student complaint that far too many dons are over-interested in research and look on their students as mere conveniences, without whose annoying presence they would be unable to indulge in it. This is undoubtedly true in certain cases, which brings us on to the second qualification, that under the new dispensation the bad don can be very bad indeed.

Not that there were not many bad dons in the past, more devoted to bookishness and port than to the needs of their undergraduates. There were plenty of them; that was one of the major deficiencies of the old system. But their effect was one of total absence rather than of doing their job badly. Every employer is saddled with long-established, inefficient employees whom for various reasons he cannot sack, but whom he blesses for absenteeism because they cannot throw spanners into the works from their homes. In the modern university, however, everybody has his job to do, no matter how inefficiently he may actually do it. The bad don of today has, therefore, become an active menace rather than the passive nuisance his nineteenth-century fore-runner contrived to be.

The good don is not simply a good teacher in his own subject; he is a good academic therapist able to stimulate in his students the natural, but often latent, inclination towards inquiry into other fields of know-ledge related to, but not an essential part of, their own immediate academic purposes. This is not a new donnish skill, but it is met with much more frequently, largely because of the new emphasis on breadth of study but also because of the modern don's closer personal involve-ment in matters that lie outside his own specialism. The growth of this trend has been pure gain. The inherent cohesion of all branches of study was being lost sight of long before the modern demand for specialists imposed itself. Apart from a few prestigious but difficult mixed courses like Greats, departmental barriers were hardening and the generalist was being ousted by the man of narrow interests and blinkered viewpoint. One of the major contributions of the new universities is their experi-mentation in ways and means of broadening academic horizons. They have not yet achieved any spectacular success, but they point the way. Perhaps somewhere there is in the making a new Bacon—or, better still, a new Thomas Browne—who will identify and define the true academic response to the technological challenge and put our latter-day schoolmen in their place while still preserving the essential humanism of a liberal education.

There is also a closer sense of identity between don and student. We shall deal with this in much greater detail in Chapter Eleven; for the moment it is sufficient to say that while some of the consequences are deplorable the better seem to outweigh the worse. A university must be a co-operative enterprise. What, in computer language, is called reacting to the student feedback is, in less technological terms, no more than understanding and meeting student needs. The modern don is better at finding out what makes his students tick. When presented with militants' 'demands' he can be just as baffled and bemused as any industrial relations officer confronted by a delegation of Trotskyist shop stewards— 'What, in God's name, do they mean by "opportunities to express our legitimate personalities"?'—but these are minority extravagances. When it comes to face-to-face discussion between the average tutor and the average student, there is a fruitful two-way dialogue that was all too rare as little as fifty years ago.

Nor does the process of learning and discovery seem to have been harmed by the abandonment of monasticism. On the contrary, there has been a succession of great leaps forward. The average don has become less of a dilettante and far more of a professional—which, of course, the best dons always were. The trouble in the past was that they were proportionately far fewer. Now, more and more salients are being driven into the frontier.

So much for the credit balance. The bad don is still with us, and dons are like little girls—when they are bad they are horrid. Permissiveness, or, to use a more familiar and less pejorative word, freedom, is simply a matter of allowing a choice between going to heaven and going to hell. The libertarian believes that the majority will ultimately opt for heaven, but he accepts that those who opt for hell will be a confounded nuisance, even a menace. Recent university experience shows this to be a pretty fair assessment. There are few checks on the behaviour of the modern don. He is much more his own master than most other professional men. Even the economic sanction that keeps most noses to the grindstone is for him a temptation to neglect his proper work and engage in more profitable activities on the side. The fact that so few give in to it to any substantial degree is a testimonial to the quality of the academic profession as a whole, but those who do are a dead loss, both to their students and to their university.

Neglect of teaching duties was less important in the not so very distant days when clocks were conveniences and not masters. Staff/student ratios were higher; there was more room for the idle don, who was able to pursue his fancy without harm to anyone or anything but himself and his academic reputation. Things are very different today when a good degree is, if not a matter of life and death, at least thought to be a passport to a promising job in a first-class firm. Students demand more attention from increasingly overworked dons, and their complaint that their teachers are idle, while unfair to the great majority, is thoroughly justified by the behaviour of some. 'They just look on us as a convenience,' one student said to me. 'If it wasn't for us students they wouldn't have all their nice cushy jobs to come to.' This shaft was directed against a young history lecturer who was currently chiefly concerned with his work as a local councillor and with the task of reinvigorating his party's constituency association. He was never to be found on the campus in the evenings or at weekends, and only at sporadic intervals during what were generally accepted to be university working hours. He was adept at altering tutorials at the last minute, leaving a hastily scribbled note—'Come at 11.30 Tuesday instead. Sorry.'—pinned to his door without any consideration for the student's convenience, and had a deplorable habit of saving time by lumping three or four tutorials together into a kind of extempore seminar irrespective of the needs of each individual student.

There are quite a number like him at Bolderdale; for instance, Gregory Helpmate in the Department of Economics. His trouble is uxorious rather than political, and his time is mainly devoted to the domestic chores inherent in having to look after a growing family and a constantly pregnant wife. His specialism is cost benefit analysis, which for him is quite obviously a theoretical not an applied science, unless he has proved to his own satisfaction that family allowances are not subject to the law of diminishing returns. His small house in University Village is bursting at the seams; he cannot invite his students to see him there, nor can he leave it in the evenings because of the chores. He lectures on classical economic theory, and in intervals between nappy washing and wife comforting, struggles to develop his thesis on the costing procedures of the recent Labour Government. His students mean very little in his life.

Professor George Browne is an entirely different kind of bad don. He pays excessive attention to his students, but not with what are normally considered legitimate academic objectives in view. He prides himself on being a renegade member of the university establishment, and measures his academic success by the number of renegade students he turns out. He is also a skilled university politician. Most of his professorial colleagues would be delighted to be rid of him, but getting rid of a departmental head in a state-financed university is rather like trying to disestablish an established civil servant. Little can be done about it in the absence of embezzlement, chronic alcoholism or persistent seduction. Professor George Browne is as dedicated as Savonarola, and there is no academic Inquisition to take him in hand. We shall come back to him in the next chapter. Here it is sufficient to say that he is a teacher of genius but devotes too much of his talent to teaching the wrong kind of thing. He has done more damage to academic excellence than a whole litter of Helpmates.

A third type of bad don is Dr Peter Phlogiston, a Senior Lecturer in chemistry. It is not that he is a rationalist, which is a wholly legitimate academic stance, nor that he is also a humanist, though the combination hints at a certain logical inconsistency, but that he is, like so many of his contemporaries, an inverted snob. Inverted snobbery, in the academic sense, is a direct reaction to the pressures of current egalitarian thought. Snobbery is an unpleasant, if natural, characteristic at all times, but it is perhaps a little less reprehensible when it is linked to professional mores rather than to external theory. Snobbery based on academic quality is bearable in an academic, less so in a stockbroker. Money snobbery is unbearable in virtually any circumstances, since the possession of money is not in itself evidence of any admirable quality. Inverted snobbery is even worse, because it is based on the absence of any quality at all. Madariaga points out, to the fury of many latter-day liberals, that the opposite of equality is not, as is popularly supposed, inequality; it is quality. In the context of that distinction, the inverted snob is a person of quality who seeks to identify himself with those of a lesser quality as a means of acquiring merit in the circles where he seeks recognition. It is like a priest getting drunk in a pub to show he is 'one of the boys'. The ordinary snob tries to equate himself with those the world might think better than he is, the inverted snob to equate himself with a rank and file to which he manifestly does not belong.

It would be difficult to find a more precise antithesis than that between egalitarianism and academic excellence. The latter is the be-all and end-all of a university, but for the inverted academic snob it is far less important than reducing university standards to accommodate those who would otherwise fail to gain admission.

Dr Phlogiston is a brilliant academic chemist, whose work in that field is highly praised by his contemporaries. He has, however, never been able to forgive himself his schooling at Winchester, his First at Oxford or the fact that he enjoys considerable private means (though he has still to sell all that he has and give it to the poor). He is a thin-faced, bespectacled man in his early thirties with a sharp, incisive mind and an even sharper tongue which he reserves particularly for those of his students who come from well-off homes. A socialist in politics, his first academic loyalty is to the state system of education. Nothing infuriates him more than public schoolboys who are able students. Their silver spoons should have been compensated for by downright stupidity. He gives them as little of his time as possible, preferring to devote his very considerable teaching ability to the working class student, however unpromising he may be. Not that he has many public schoolboys as students. He spends a great deal of energy on influencing admissions procedures, and fights tooth and nail for their exclusion. It is doubtful whether dons of his kind could have existed at all in an earlier age, though it is true that other forms of discrimination on academically irrelevant grounds were frequently practised. What distinguishes him as a particularly modern product is his conviction that the pursuit of learning must be subservient to a political creed that itself has no genuine academic root. There are plenty of socialist dons at Bolderdale, but only a few who rate their socialism above their academic integrity. Professor Pontifex Prime has voted Labour all his life, but it has probably never even occurred to him to ration out his academic favours on a basis of politics or class.

That Dr Phlogiston should be a foremost member of the Bolderdale branch of the Association of University Teachers almost goes without saying. The unionisation of dons, like the unionisation of students (which we shall look at in a later chapter), is a modern phenomenon. It is not a professional body like the British Medical Association or the Law Society, concerned as much with professional standards as with conditions of service, but a lobby concerned primarily with pay. No one would deny that it is a necessary organisation in a society in which academic salaries are standardised on a national scale, and in fact something like 60 per cent of dons belong to it.

A representative bargaining body is essential to virtually any form of organised activity in this age of the pressure group. Unfortunately the AUT suffers, to a greater or lesser degree from university to university, from the original sin inseparable from all such organisations—it offers an ideal instrument for the political activist who can divert it from its proper purposes to the service of his own, and can debauch it just as communists have debauched many formerly reputable trade unions. Not that the AUT is in any present danger of subversion; too many dons recognise its weakness in this respect, and valiant efforts are made to fill its tempting power vacuum with those who put academic standards ahead of political aims. They deserve more support than they get from the profession as a whole. Here and there they are moderately successful, but they are up against the almost insuperable difficulty that the academic profession is so diverse and reaches over such a vast field of endeavour that it is virtually impossible to set up any but the most general rules for it. The established learned societies are the effective guardians of professional standards. It is only on pay that all academic interests converge, and it is here that the AUT comes into its political own, commanding a large membership, which means a proportionately large income, coupled with a widespread disinclination to play an active part in the dreary grind of its practical work.[1]

At Bolderdale those with political axes of their own have won control. Meetings are usually attended by a select minority of maybe twenty-five staff members, among whom Professor George Browne and Dr Phlogiston are pre-eminent. They produce occasional flurries of resolutions on ostensibly academic topics—academic freedom, student representation, admissions procedure, examinations, grants, discipline— which, when consolidated, add up to a fairly comprehensive body of current left-wing doctrine. The Vice-Chancellor reads them dutifully and his secretary files them carefully. Professor Pontifex Prime gives them deeper thought, and has been known to refer to this one or that in characteristically scathing terms at formal meetings of the Academic Senate. Most Bolderdale staff consign them wearily to the wastepaper basket and get on with their work. Resolutions from the students' union receive much more attention.

The AUT should not be treated lightly. Its influence is considerable and very necessary within its proper sphere, but it is also a significant signpost on the road of academic development. Universities used to be highly individual and expected their members to be the same; the unit of organisation was the Common Room—or, in cases of extreme crisis, Congregation—and no student of human affairs could seriously describe a Senior Common Room as a highly organised body, except perhaps in matters of food and drink. Until quite recently there was no formal mechanism for inter-university co-operation. Today, however, we seem to be moving into a monopolistic world in which the independent unit, if it is to survive at all, will do so only on terms that will severely circumscribe its effectiveness. This applies over the whole range of effort, from industry to doctoring, and the academic world is proving an easy victim. The forced expansion of universities since the war, together with the emergence of the state as the sole paymasters of their staff, has welded the academic profession into a single entity.

[1] Mr Clive Jenkins' ASTMS (Association of Scientific, Technical and Managerial Staffs) is said to be invading the academic community, but it is not easy to get any statistics of its success so far. It is probable that most members employed by universities are technicians rather than academics.

It would be quite fair to say that universities are now well along the way to becoming industrialised, in the sense that they are being subjected to the same processes that changed craft industry into organised industry over the period from the beginning of the Industrial Revolution up to the present day. They are becoming subject to the same managerial techniques that are forcing amalgamations throughout the industrial world. On the organisational side, university independence is giving way to the Committee of Vice-Chancellors, on the staff side to the AUT and on the student side to the National Union of Students. The AUT has in effect become the collective bargaining unit of a nationalised industry, and the university teacher is becoming more and more like any other industrial employee.

At a minority of universities this has led to a staff trade union situation in which a small group of activists contrive to use the union for political purposes. It is a process that will develop. The same is true to an even greater extent among the students, as we shall see in Chapter Nine. Politics among dons, however, deserves a special chapter to itself.

CHAPTER EIGHT

University politics

Anyone who climbs the hillside of a highland glen after heavy rain and pauses in the heather to look back over the view, will become conscious of faint sounds rising from the ground beneath his feet which, as the ear becomes accustomed to them, take the form of the rippling of running water. To right and left other streams make themselves heard until the climber becomes aware that he is standing in a vast watercourse, split into tiny units by the long action of the weather on the peat between the heather roots and entirely hidden from sight by the blooming heather bells. So it is with a university. Under the apparently placid surface of academe, innumerable rivulets of secret activity are constantly whispering away. The whole place is richly, vigorously and invisibly alive with an underground life of its own.

Politics are inseparable from almost any kind of co-operative society. It takes two to make a quarrel, but wherever three are gathered together they are certain to generate some kind of political activity. From the small family unit to Parliament itself people combine and recombine in a bewildering, changing kaleidoscope of groupings in order to achieve their aims. Little Alice flatters her father into taking her side in a tussle with her mother about a new dress; schoolboys form secret societies; businessmen intrigue for high posts; the balance of power on the Parochial Church Council is decisive on the form churchmanship is to take; the local dramatic society, the board of directors, the divisional HQ, the newspaper chapel are all seedbeds of politics, every bit as much as the local Conservative Association or the smoking room of the House of Commons. Factions take form under the stress of conflicting interests, split or amalgamate as new interests dictate, strengthen or collapse according to their success or failure. Expertise in one's job may be the basis of advancement, but political skill is its handmaid.

Outside government there is no more fertile field for the practice of politics than a university. Even under the most carefully drafted of charters its organisation is necessarily loose. Dons cannot be disciplined except in the broadest terms; they can be discouraged from seducing their students or stealing each other's books, but by and large these are not normal academic activities. In their professional lives they are remarkably free. They are, moreover, actively encouraged to take a political stance since they are all in one way or another concerned—if not directly as members of court, council or senate, then within their own departments or on interdisciplinary boards of studies—in university government. All staff members enjoy some degree of power and are provided with institutional means of exercising it.

The physical structure of a university also lends itself to the practice of politics. A great deal of shop is talked in Senior Common Rooms and much of it is political in the university sense: Who is in line for next year's history appointment? What is the Vice-Chancellor going to do about the library? Can this or that motion be carried in the senate? Is it true that the professor of English has put in his resignation? What cuts are going to be proposed as a result of UGC stinginess? How is the rumoured grant from Omnium Limited going to be shared out?

The real meat of the matter lies in these last two questions—cuts and grants. They are important sources of redundancy or advancement, not by any means the only sources but the ones most open to manipulation. Not that dons are more mercenary than anyone else, but their academic ambitions are passions that go to the depths of their souls. The pursuit of truth is a dominating master. Grants to pursue a particular avenue of research, finance for the enlargement of a department or threats of withdrawal of funds are competed for or resisted with a political skill that would do credit to a cabinet faced by an impecunious and parsimonious Chancellor of the Exchequer in a period of retrenchment. Nor are the ideologists, both those who are anxious to limit new appointments to dons of their own party political cast of thought and those who seek more legitimate academic ends, behindhand in political manoeuvre. In fact it is almost impossible for a don not to be, in some degree, also a politician. There are some who take to it like ducks to water—the despatches of *Mercurius Oxeniensis* offer a fascinating collection of case studies[1]—but even the most placid dweller in an ivory tower is capable from time to time of becoming involved in some highly devious political entanglement.

The highly political don is instantly recognisable. For one thing, his telephone never stops ringing. Let me give some examples from Bolderdale. On one of my visits there I spent an hour with an eminent don who taught philosophy. We were supposed to be discussing books on that

[1] *The Letters of Mercurius Oxeniensis*, John Murray, London, 1970. These witty accounts of Oxford's underlife deserve study by any reader who would like an inside view of the more sophisticated side of university politics—and they offer as much instruction as pleasure, which is saying much.

subject, but I doubt if we spent twenty minutes all told on our immediate business. The telephone was too active. Big matters were apparently afoot, but I could only glean a one-sided and somewhat mystifying idea of them. 'My dear X, how nice of you to ring. How's your poor wife's ankle? . . . Yes, I'm sure it's very tedious for you. I expect I'll manage to slip along, though I'm a bit pressed—a Wittgenstein article for the *Quarterly*. Overdue, of course. . . . Yes, I imagined that would be your line. I can't say I wholly agree, but I expect we'll reach some *modus vivendi*. . . . No, I could hardly go as far as that. I don't honestly think that the V-C would like it that way. . . . Well, I'll try and get there. Two-thirty, isn't it? . . . Thank you, my regards to your poor wife.' Or again, 'Oh, hello Roger. . . . Yes, of course I'll be there. So will C. . . . Oh, D. . . . has decided to come, has he? Good. He was rather doubtful about it—a postponed tutorial. . . . Admirable. . . . I'm afraid we can be pretty certain W. . . . and Y. . . . will both make it. . . . No, I think we should avoid a show-down at this stage—play it gently. Phillippi isn't on us yet. . . . All right, I'll see you in the bar at twelve forty-five. . . . The meeting's at two, isn't it? Good-bye.'

Which only goes to show that even philosophers thoroughly enjoy the game of academic cops and robbers. The only clue I picked up as to the gravamen of the dispute was a remark thrown out during our truncated business discussion. 'My own guess is that the philosophy of sociology is going to attract a good deal of interest. In fact we're thinking of starting a special course on it here. Oddly enough, Wittgenstein has some theorems that are quite relevant. There's a bit of opposition, naturally. No one likes philosophy applied to his own subject—theologians, historians, scientists. Still, we often get our way.' I was not surprised.

A Bolderdale politician of a different type is Professor John Doughtman, Dean of the School of Environment, which is his passion and for which one gets the impression he would gladly lay down his life. Tall, good-looking, with an Epstein jaw ('Oh, I flew a Spitfire,' he says casually when occasion warrants), he was the founder of the School and has guided it brilliantly through all the shoals that surround any new academic venture superimposed on a traditional structure. He is a member of every university committee of any account, and his finger is never very far from the trigger in case more sophisticated methods should fail. He shows true prime ministerial qualities where the administration of the School is concerned; he is an admirable butcher. The results, shown by the success of his School and the reputation of Bolderdale, have been most satisfactory.

Theoretically, politics are the art of cohesion; in practice they often turn out to be a source of disruption. What the university gains out of this swings and roundabouts situation is all too often offset by the damage done on the side. Passions always run high in the academic world, if only because cool, pragmatic solutions do not always commend themselves to those who are chiefly concerned with theory and speculation and tend to rate value judgements above the dictates of common sense. In a small community divisions of opinion run deep, and leave a permanent mark. In mediaeval days this was often the source of new universities being established. Oxford is supposed to have hived off from Paris in precisely this way, and a similar case can be put for the belief that Cambridge broke away from Oxford. There was also an unsuccessful stampede from Oxford to Stamford, but the experiment failed. Today's projected independent university is a faintly similar phenomenon.

Academic politics today are no less sharp, no less bitter, than they were in the more monastic days of the nineteenth century, but they are more real in the sense that they reflect concern with what are essentially practical matters. As in any practical political community, they reflect the three basic political postures—conservation, progressivism and liberalism. Conservatives, like the poor, will always be with us; there must, in any society, be a body of privilege resistant to any change that fails to increase that privilege, either for purely selfish motives or out of the sheer inertia that accompanies a sense of well-being and security. Progressives, too, there must always be; they are found mainly among the underprivileged, but also, though to a lesser degree, among those privileged who are primarily moved by genuine idealism rather than by the logic of personal need. The trouble about progressivism is that it is more closely concerned with raising the anchor than with charting a course or ensuring that the engines are efficient and the fuel supply adequately guaranteed. Whenever progressive elements win control they are apt to find their early unity collapsing under the pressure of having to decide which way to go. The theorists quarrel among themselves while the pragmatists adjust policy to the compulsions of the politically possible and eventually produce a new *status quo* which in due course forms the basis of a new conservatism. The relation between these two attitudes is linear. Between but above them, like the uppermost angle of a triangle, one finds the liberals (writing the word with a deliberate small 'l'), a much abused term by which I mean those who accept not only the need for change but also the need to base it on those features of their social inheritance that still have an essential part to play in the immediate future. Perhaps the most precise political term to describe it is Whiggism. All three groups are to be found in universities as much as in the House of Commons.

Academic conservatism draws its strength from the academic establishments, and its main effect is to create a barrier to academic innovation and experiment. Dons have their favourite courses, methods of examination and forms of tuition; and they also have strong vested interests in the system in which they have found a place for themselves, in the facilities for research they enjoy, in their orderly progress up the ladder of promotion. Oxford finally produced its new joint course in economics and engineering only after herculean labours to overcome the deeply held conviction of both economists and engineers that neither could give up one jot or tittle of the courses they were already teaching. No one, the protagonists maintained, could understand the essentials of either discipline unless subjected to its complete curriculum.

Academic progressives want to sweep away most of the existing system and, broadly speaking, to replace it with something new based on current demands for equality and permissiveness. They are by no means agreed on practical proposals but they tend to favour anything that shows contempt for the *status quo*, whether this is a lowering of standards to accommodate a wider range of student, a shift of power balance within the constitutional organs of university government or straight encouragement of student revolt. They are to be found mostly among those with a personal chip on their shoulders, though not a few are established members of the *ancien régime* with the same guilt complex that brought many French aristocrats into the body of the Revolution.

Liberals are more numerous in academic circles than in the world at large, as might be expected in communities mainly concerned with analytical and experimental study. Progressives label them right-wing because they are trying to hold hard to the traditional academic virtues. Conservatives look on them as dangerous progressives because they threaten existing vested interests by challenging their continuing relevance and validity. This does not mean that they are colourless fence-sitters. They are, more exactly, the spearhead of the academic attack both on the fatuities of society and on the complacency which makes some universities drift into complete irrelevance to that society.

The subject matter of current university politics can be classed under several heads. There are, for instance, the straight pork-barrel politics concerned with how available resources are to be used. This has come to assume greater importance in these days of economic stringency and increasing political control, but it has also found a wider field of operation than the domestic academic community, because financial control no longer rests with the governmental organs of each individual university. As we have seen, the UGC is increasingly becoming the dominant decision maker on how funds derived from public sources shall be used, and also how they shall be allocated as between university and university. Parallel with this development, the new Committee of Vice-Chancellors, which treats with the UGC on behalf of the totality of universities, is becoming more of a power mechanism. Although very few academics can aspire to membership of either of these bodies, there are methods of influencing them in addition to the normal methods of give and take that operated when each university was master of its own destiny. The more of a public figure a don becomes, or, to put it less politely, the more of a public nuisance he can make of himself, the more he will be listened to. This is one of the factors, in addition to the straight financial one, that has led so many dons to the microphone and the TV cameras. It is also a source of vitamin injection into inter-university groupings such as the Association of University Teachers. On the whole, however, pork-barrel politics are played by individuals or at the highest by departments, researchers seeking the cash for new laboratories or departmental heads hoping for extra staff. It can be a cut-throat business, usually played out with a suavity and polished charm that disguises but does not limit its razor-sharp quality.

The sharpest in-fighting is reserved for the politics of academic ideology, which have assumed monumental importance now that higher education has become a matter of public policy instead of a private exercise for those interested in it. The lines are fairly tightly drawn: the conservatives determined to resist all change other than change directed towards their own benefit, the progressives eager for the brave new world they have still failed to define and the liberals infuriating both by putting forward concrete proposals for reform. Broadly speaking the battle is waged between élitism and egalitarianism, which is no more than the centuries-old struggle between the haves and the have-nots, with the liberals firmly entrenched on the élitist side but opening their minds to some of the more reasonable egalitarian claims. This triangle of forces stimulates a running war in all the committees concerned with such subjects as admissions, appointments, examination boards, student/staff relations, student discipline, curriculum changes—anything, indeed, that has a bearing on the élitist-egalitarian conflict. Most universities are affected by it: some, mercifully, only lightly; a few dangerously diseased. The universities which have suffered but survive owe their good fortune chiefly to the tact of their vice-chancellors, the political skill of men like Professor Pontifex Prime at Bolderdale and a reciprocal balance on the part of those like Professor George Browne who are well aware of how far they can go before political wisdom dictates calling a halt. The real dangers come from the politically active but politically inept extremists on either side.

A frequent source of disaster is the practice, happily rare, of by-passing the normal constitutional channels—committees, council and senate —and enlisting the sympathy of student activists. In the nature of things, this usually occurs in support of the egalitarian cause. As we shall see when we come to look at the students, there *are* conservative activists among them, but they are incapable of effectively militant organisation, whereas those on the left seem to have imbibed with their mothers' milk a gift for political combination. There are, unhappily, dons who see them as a supporting arm in their own political cause, and do not scruple to mobilise them. Whatever else may be achieved by this tactic, it is the academic community that suffers in the end. It is one thing for dons to engage in political warfare among themselves over matters for which they carry a degree of responsibility, but the use of student pressure to gain a victory can only result in exaggerating the 'we and they' attitude to the point at which the community is split along lines of status or class, a situation which can destroy the atmosphere of tolerance on which the life of any voluntary community depends.

An army formation maintains its unity through leadership based on military law. In a university, discipline can only be preserved by a spirit of mutual acceptance and a sense of common purpose. The student disturbances over 'confidential files' at Warwick in 1969, which received strong support from a number of staff members, offer an illustration of the danger. In Birmingham the following year efforts were made to enlist student support in favour of a proposed staff appointment which had previously been rejected by the constitutional appointment authority.

The third field of politics is not academic at all, but national. It is often said that one function of universities should be to take a stand on public affairs, but it would be hard to find any sound justification for this. A university should reflect many views, not a single one. There have been occasions of great stress, when a university has intervened, as a university, in the national political process, but there have been very few—for instance Oxford's support for the loyalist cause in the Civil War. There have been other occasions when a single group has been assumed, incorrectly, to be speaking for the university as a whole; Oxford again provides an example in the Union Debate in the middle 1930s when it was resolved that 'This House will not fight for King and Country'. This was an effective political intervention with wide repercussions on national events, but it represented no more than a majority view within a minority group of students. There is a clear distinction between an intervention by a group within a university and the idea that it is one of the functions of a university to make its corporate opinion felt in the process of reaching a national consensus. The former is, within limits, a natural right and a healthy exercise in democratic action; the latter is a by-product of modern democratic practice whereby efforts are made to mobilise every possible source of pressure on one side or the other of the national political struggle. The political activists argue: 'It is up to Bolderdale to take a line on Vietnam'—or comprehensive schools, or the Common Market (or pollution, permissiveness, productivity, participation, privacy, pornography—or any other of the trendy Ps). From the activist's point of view, the intellectual standing of the university makes it an unusually valuable ally if its influence can be mobilised on the side of this or that nostrum, especially in these days of mass communication when student protest is both news for the Press and spectacle for television. Politicians have always interested themselves in universities in the past, but as recruiting grounds rather than as allies; the political clubs were important sources of future strength. Today their interest has increased, but the aim is now as much to obtain a good public platform for current political battles and directly to enlist in the power game the authority carried in their name. It is not only in matters of finance that the politicians contrive to interfere in university affairs.

When, in 1970, a group of Cambridge student militants invaded the Garden House Hotel and committed mayhem on a number of diners there with whose political views they disagreed, there was, according to newspaper reports, a don stationed on a neighbouring balcony overlooking the scene who offered them enthusiastic encouragement through a loudspeaker. This, let it be said, was abnormal: it is rare for dons to participate directly in student protest—they prefer the roles of *éminences grises*. But the fact that it could happen at all is an indication of the absurd degree to which national politics are impinging on the academic community.

If such trends are allowed to develop, the outlook for the universities will be bleak. The causes are deep-seated and, even in the case of strictly academic disputes, are rooted in a national debate rather than in any local issue. Politics have come to be organised on a national scale and the national centres of political power are laying siege to every local power centre on a scale that could never have been approached when news and views could be disseminated only relatively slowly over relatively small areas. In one sense improved communications are, or should be, aids to personal initiative, but they also carry inherent dangers, chief of which in this context is their centralising influence. The mass circulation newspaper, radio and television all help the demagogue to enlarge his constituency, and radio and television especially, both being near-monopolies, offer him a far more effective medium than can be achieved by the printed or spoken word, as well as placing severe limits on the variety of opinion that can be expressed. It is not surprising that control of mass communications should be the first target in a *coup d'état*. Mass communications also help to produce a sense of identity between widely separated groups, and have been an important factor in developing the unionisation of students which, as we shall see, is bearing fruit in an entirely new concept, defined by no less an authority than Sir Eric Ashby, the Master of Clare College, Cambridge, as 'The Student Estate'.

The combination of the 'instant politics' of TV with the developing sense of identity between student activists (and staff activists as well) in widely separated institutions has laid the formerly enclosed individual universities open to the full impact of national political forces; and since education itself has become one of the main arenas of political conflict the universities are being caught up in the national political vendetta. This may be good for the politicians, but is totally irrelevant and inimical to the university purposes of learning and discovery, and can do them nothing but harm in the not-so-long run. Although a majority of dons are aware of this danger, they find themselves forced into a defensive posture by a minority and driven into spending an undue proportion of their time on what are essentially non-academic activities. As a result, the proper work of the institution suffers; the learning process is disrupted, and the calm and time for reflection needed to stimulate the process becomes all the more difficult to achieve. The most immediate sufferers are those students—a majority—who take their work seriously and look to the successful outcome of their studies to equip them for their future careers; but in the long run it is the whole academic community that is hurt.

I am not arguing that politics should be exiled from the university. On the contrary, in the earlier part of this chapter I made it plain that political activity is inseparable from academic life. Nor am I arguing that it should be confined to academic politics; it is right that both staff and students should interest themselves in national affairs and take up, if they wish, a passionate stance on whatever view they believe to be right. But the means for that are at hand—Common Rooms, debating societies and political clubs provide all that is necessary. It is quite another matter that the university as a whole should be dragged into the political arena and made to play a part utterly alien to its nature and damaging to its future. To some degree the fault lies with the politicians, to some degree with the less responsible dons and to some degree with the student activists. Of the three, I should say that the over-political dons are the most culpable element; they carry the heaviest responsibility for the welfare of their institutions. Students have their responsibilities to their institution as well, but they are diminished when student protest is encouraged by seniors to whom the student has a right to look for guidance. The politicians are merely plying their trade, and one would not expect them to do otherwise, however much one might regret it. It is not only to the universities that they bring disruption.

I have devoted some considerable space to this problem because it highlights one of the most serious internal weaknesses of the academic community: its dependence on self-discipline in an age when self-discipline is more apt to be sneered at than encouraged. In a sense the whole community shares in the responsibility—administrators, dons and students all alike. A university lives by the spirit it generates from within its own resources, and if it is unable to invoke that spirit to greater or lesser degree in all of its members, it will progressively fail. However many Firsts it may produce, however high the quality of its research, it will eventually fall into decline if it cannot inspire loyalty among its members. External pressures—from government, from politicians, from a general public malaise, even from other universities—may provide the reasons for its failure, but they cannot provide an excuse.

In the end, however, it all comes back to the dons. It is they who should set the tone. The administrators are, or should be, their servants. The students should be able to look to them for guidance. However many good dons there may be in a university, a small proportion of inadequate ones can frustrate their efforts. The Duke of Wellington was reported to have said that the hard-working but stupid officer must be got rid of at all cost. It is the same with dons. Those who are stupid enough to want to politicise their universities and earnest and dogged enough to devote to that purpose the loyalties and abilities that ought to be given to strengthening their community fabric, turning out scholars and attacking the frontiers of knowledge, are a menace to their institutions. Loyalty and self-control, as in every other form of communal endeavour, are the key to a good university, and the more strongly the universities are under attack from the social fashions of the day, the greater is their need of them.

CHAPTER NINE

The changing student

The student body is not only the largest part of any university community, it is also what distinguishes it from a research institution and keeps it in close touch with the world of the rising generation. Only a small proportion of students have made their own careers within the academic community, though large numbers of them have carried away a love of learning and a habit of studious inquiry into the parish, hospital, classroom, laboratory, law office, political circle, industry or drawing office in which their subsequent lives have been spent. Most students spend three years at a British university (though in Scotland four is more normal). The majority arrive as raw recruits, knowing as little about what lies ahead of them as the conscript does about what is involved in military service. When they leave, a surprisingly high proportion of them have, like a somewhat smaller proportion of conscripts, acquired an entirely new attitude to life and its problems. At the critical age of adolescence they have been subjected to a wholly adult experience, coming to it still wet from the egg of schooling and leaving it equipped, in greater or lesser degree in proportion to their response to the challenge, to play an effective part in the affairs of the world. There are, of course, exceptions, young men and women who, for innate reasons or because of the influence of their parents or school-teachers, have matriculated to university fully equipped to be members of the academic community from the beginning, but they are very few in number. To many, the sudden transition can prove quite an alarming experience.

Nevertheless, transient, unskilled and ignorant of academic life though its members may be on first arrival, the student body as a whole is the heart of any university. The devoted researcher may resent their claims on his time but he depends on them. Without the students he would have no laboratory, no library, no salary to keep body and soul together. In a very true sense dons are the servants of their students, and the best dons are very well aware of the fact. They are, however, highly skilled servants, and they can only do their job if their skills and authority are recognised by those they teach. In a later chapter we shall be dealing with don/student relations. Here we are more concerned with what kind of people the students are, where they come from, why they come to the university at all and what they hope to get out of it.

In the opening chapter of this book we looked at some of the changes that have taken place in the student body over the last hundred years. Briefly, the change can be summed up as a vast increase in numbers, the opening of universities to women and a certain broadening of the class basis. What we are concerned with now is the changes in attitude that have flowed from these changes in form.

First, let us dispose of one change that is often alleged to have taken place, or to be in the course of taking place, but which is not in fact taking place at all. University students, it is said, no longer form an élite or privileged group, no longer enjoy advantages withheld from others. Although the number of students has increased many-fold, and although they are drawn from a wider class basis, they still enjoy a privileged position in so far as they receive a finish to their education that others do not. They are not *better* people—not morally, not in terms of social class, not in any ultimate or absolute sense—but they are given a chance of equipping themselves more fully for the business of life. The graduate enjoys rank and status, if not always esteem.

An élite group is not necessarily a small group, though normally it is a minority of the whole. White-skinned people are an élite in South Africa; but so they are in England where the number of people with coloured skins is comparatively small. The distinguishing features of an élite are the enjoyment of particular advantages and the status that goes with them; some measure of mutual recognition between them, and of common interest; and awareness of these advantages of status and common interest. The formation of élites is a natural and inevitable development in any form of society and cannot be avoided under any method of social organisation yet evolved. The egalitarian aim of eliminating them always boils down in the end to enlarging them. It is for the common good that they should be enlarged; the objection to élites is not that they exist, but that admission to them is unfairly withheld from those who have the ability to belong. There will always be differences in quality and ability, courage and virtue, health and genes. What is important is that no one should be artificially deprived by man-made barriers from developing to the full such of these qualities as he does actually enjoy.

Admission to a university is a privilege. It confers the right to the highest form of education yet devised, the opportunity of an intellectually and spiritually superior quality of life and the prospect of higher earning ability. These rewards are by no means confined to university graduates, but they are normally much harder to come by in any other way. In

Britain, this privilege was closely circumscribed until 1945. Today the gates have been thrown open to more than five times the 1945 number. They could and should be thrown open wider still. But if universities are to maintain their quality (and it is essential to the welfare of society that they should do so) admission to them must be limited to those who are best qualified to profit from what they have to offer. The present British system is, in theory at any rate, well designed to achieve that purpose. A minimal qualification is set, and it is left to each university to select its students from among those so qualified. The result is, on the whole, a high quality of student. To be accepted by a university today is a badge of honour—or perhaps one should say a provisional badge of honour, for the university course has still to be successfully completed.

University students are, therefore, from the most callow freshman or freshwoman to the most sophisticated aspirant to a doctorate, members of a carefully selected and well-qualified élite. Errors are made, of course; and the well qualified are sometimes rejected, the useless admitted; even the best of admissions procedures slips up from time to time. Nevertheless, most students have earned their place, and the overwhelming majority of them in due course justify the opinion of their selectors. So, in considering the place of students within the academic community, we begin with the fact that the majority of them are there by virtue of their own qualities and have the ability to make a personal contribution to the life of the university. But they *are* an élite.

This was not always the case. In the early mediaeval universities most of the students were probably there because they had a deep desire for learning and the will to go in search of it. It was a much prized rarity. But later—in, say, seventeenth-century Oxford or Cambridge (Scotland was still at the mediaeval stage in that respect)—this was less true. By then it had become fashionable to be a student, and fashion was largely limited to the upper classes. In the eighteenth century the situation tended to grow worse. Dr Johnson enjoyed his time at Oxford and bitterly regretted the poverty that forced him back to Litchfield, but he seems to have been worse than idle while he was there, and the whole atmosphere was lax to the point of neglect. It was not until the nineteenth-century advances in natural science and technology that the universities began to claw their way back up the ladder of academic respectability, but even then status, or in its absence wealth, remained the key to entry. Younger sons of the nobility and landed families destined for the Church, and the sons of rich bourgeois aiming at the professions or perhaps simply at personal contact with the aristocracy, still formed a sizeable part of the student body as the century drew to a close, but the general intellectual quality of students had been rising fast, with Oxford specialising in the humanities and Cambridge in the more novel disciplines. The social mix had become less one-sided and academic purpose was stronger. In Scotland, where in spite of ups and downs the universities had clung more closely to the traditions of pure learning, student numbers were growing rapidly and the range of studies with increasing speed. At the same time, the new civic universities were bringing the opportunity for higher education within the range of the new middle classes thrown up by the Industrial Revolution.

Up to the beginning of the second world war, however, the student body remained a *small* élite. Fees were high and scholarships limited in number, and in England at any rate the urge towards higher education was slow to percolate. What was changing was the motivation of the majority of those who did go to university. This was in part due to the admission of women students, most of whom were untouched by the subsidiary motives that attracted many men—sport, social purpose or political ambition. They were pure learners and brought to the universities a more serious approach to study than a high proportion of the men had done. But this was also due to the growing emphasis which the nineteenth century had placed on the university degree as a qualification for various walks of life. Previously the vocational purposes of the universities had been largely confined to the ancient professions, but by 1900 they had also become the gateway to engineering and science, to the Civil and Foreign Services, to the pro-consular posts offered by the Colonial and India Offices and to the higher posts in education. Universities were no longer catering solely to the traditional professions, but were becoming the key to middle class advancement.

During my years at Oxford (1929–32) the student body was predominantly middle class. The *Zuleika Dobson* period had ended. There were many, many more Noakeses and far fewer Dukes and Marrabys, who were mostly to be found in Christ Church, a college which has somehow contrived even in this new age of the 1970s to retain more than a smattering of its earlier social distinction. Sport was still a pre-eminent interest, and the old Oxford student *Weltanschaung*, which had nothing to do with the university's true excellence, still hung about the place like a miasma. Women students, though far less numerous than today, were much in evidence, but were known as 'undergraduettes', a diminutive that would have enraged a Women's Lib movement had there been one. Social intercourse was hedged in by fierce restrictions. Such feminism as existed took the form of aping male practice, and was severely frowned on by the authorities of the women's colleges. In a broadcast some years ago Miss Dilys Powell told a frightening story of how she was rusticated after she had been found climbing into Somerville late one night by an irate female don. An undergraduette could only visit an undergraduate in his room if chaperoned by another undergraduette, and within strictly limited hours. Today the situation is completely changed. There is no longer any such thing as an undergraduette; there are only students and any formal attempt to distinguish between them on grounds of sex would be regarded as a kind of racism. Personal relations have been transformed. As Dacre Balsdon has pointed out in *Oxford Now and Then*,[1] every Jack now has his Jill. They can be seen any day walking hand-in-hand down the Broad and performing a ritual ballet which involves a succulent embrace every thirty yards or so.

For all that, the women are still on the whole more serious students than the men, and contribute more to the stability of the academic life of the university. Even among the men, however, there is an increasingly serious attitude towards study. Oxford students have less money than they did, which means fewer opportunities for distraction, and are more keenly aware that their futures depend on the quality of their academic achievements.

The social mix of students, both at Oxbridge and elsewhere, has changed only slightly since the 1930s. University students are still predominantly middle class. The overall proportion of working class students, including those in the recently upgraded technical colleges, is, as far as the inadequate current statistics show, possibly as high as 25%. This is very unpleasant to the egalitarians, but the cause is fairly obvious. The first reason for going to a university at all is that one is brought up in a milieu that itself encourages the idea. This does not mean that one's parents must have been to a university, but that the home atmosphere encourages a desire for knowledge. Children who are brought up in a home where there is a good supply of books of a more than purely fictional kind quickly learn to enjoy reading and get the habit of acquiring knowledge. On the whole, books are comparatively scarce in working class homes and television is far too ephemeral to be an effective substitute. The wonder is that as many as 25% actually conceive a desire for higher education. If the egalitarians would only base their activities on the recognition that the key to a still wider diffusion of academic status lies in homes and schools rather than with university admissions committees, they would be performing a much more useful function.

The real changes in the nature of the student body boil down to two, one of purpose and outlook and one of status. The purpose of the average

[1] Duckworth, London, 1970. This book is strongly recommended to every undergraduate—and to every don, for that matter.

undergraduate today is much more frankly vocational than it used to be: it is more to fit himself for a job than to acquire scholarly sophistication. Although universities always had their vocational aspects, and had come to put more emphasis on them as science and technology advanced, it would be fair to say that a very high proportion of serious students still made pure learning their goal in the 1930s. Today most students have more worldly aims, and treat their time at university as an investment rather than an intellectual privilege. To a very large degree this is a by-product of the change in the economic status of the middle classes, through which salary has come to replace property as the main source of middle class income. Inheritance has ceased to be a serious factor in the lives of most young people from middle class homes. They know that they will have to stand on their own feet from the time their education comes to an end, and that their success or failure at university may very largely determine their future. Society offers very little comfort to the dilettante nowadays.

One aspect of this change is the growth of specialisation, particularly in science and technology. This is encouraged by the school system, which tends to enforce specialisation from the age of fifteen or even fourteen. Although it is a trend that many universities are trying to fight through the promotion of interdisciplinary studies, the remedy is only partially successful and is likely to remain so until university qualifications for specialist courses have been relaxed sufficiently to include some non-technical 'A' levels. A vicious spiral is in progress. To meet university qualification requirements the schools enforce narrower specialisation on their pupils, with the result that new students are less and less qualified for general studies, while to meet the demands of school-leavers universities are compelled to provide increasing opportunities for narrow specialists.

This is proving a self-defeating policy. Employers of graduates are becoming overtly more dissatisfied with the end product. They need specialists, but specialists who have acquired considerable knowledge outside their own specialisms. The pure specialist, unless he is outstandingly brilliant, is unlikely to make great progress in later life, and can all too easily find himself out of date. It is the specialist with a broader background or the generalist with an understanding of how specialists think and work who is best able to compete with the pressures of modern industrial life.

Perhaps some inkling of this has communicated itself to the undergraduate and even the sixth-former, for recent years have seen an almost instinctive revolt against science and technology. Many university places in these subjects remain unfilled, while there is an increasing demand for the social sciences and the more relevant humanities. Some university-watchers put it down to a lazy search for soft options or to an almost morbid preoccupation with a disintegrating society, but I feel more inclined to see it as an example of instinctive self-protection, an almost biological reaction against excess. Scientists and technologists will be in increasing demand at the lower levels of industry, but it is highly questionable whether the present system of higher education is producing the kind of scientists and technologists who will be best fitted to climb to the upper ranges. I have acquired considerable admiration for the average university student of today, who seems very determined to get the best out of his opportunities. If his schooling had done more to prepare him for university life, as distinct from university admission, he would get even more out of them than he does. In that sense, those from public and grammar schools still enjoy a very considerable advantage; but the whole student body, from whatever kind of school, is, I should say, of higher quality and sophistication than it has ever been.

The change in student status has been even more remarkable; but it has brought disadvantages in its train. Some of the disadvantages will be examined in the chapter on don/student relations, and some in the chapter on protest in universities, but it is necessary that here we should look at the broad elements of what has happened. In their recent book on the subject,[1] Sir Eric Ashby and Dr Mary Anderson develop the theory that a new 'student estate' has emerged. Precisely what they mean by the term is not very clear. The words would normally imply a new, coherent, self-aware power in the land, equivalent to Church, Lords and Commons. It was the power it exercised that caused the Press to be called the 'fourth estate', and the trade union leadership has climbed up to a similar position, but students have very little power. They frequently make the headlines and they know how to supply television with good visual copy but their influence is ephemeral and not at all likely to increase except in marginal matters. They could more accurately be described as a pressure group; this in itself is enough of a break with tradition to make it worth considering in some detail.

Universities are hives of individualism, and their members are not normally prone to collective action. The comparative failure of the AUT to become a pressure group outside the very limited field of salary scales is a good example of the difficulties of organising academic opinion. One would have thought it would prove even more difficult to organise students, whose student days are brief but whose ultimate aims are far less alike than those of the senior members who have made the

[1] *The Rise of the Student Estate*, Macmillan, London, 1971.

universities their career. On the contrary, it has proved far easier, and the reasons for this deserve to be explored.

The change we have just been examining in student attitudes is one of the main reasons. Students are more serious and more aware of the outside world than they were. They are also at a highly mimetic age and tend to copy the methods of people older than themselves, even while professing to despise the older generation. This is an era of collective action in which pressure groups proliferate in almost every walk of life from season-ticket holder associations to the TUC and the CBI. It would be more surprising if students failed to try to follow an existing adult pattern than if they ignored it. While they remain students they have certain interests in common, mostly financial, but in some measure academic and social as well, and these interests tend to be common to most students in most universities. Probably the most successful initiatives of the National Union of Students have been its organisation of cheap travel for students, and its lobbying for increased grants and better residences. It has certainly made membership of the Union a worthwhile asset.

To have common interests, however, is quite different from the ability to create an organisation to exploit them, let alone becoming a new power in society. Until quite recently no serious effort was made to organise students on a national scale. A certain amount was achieved within individual universities, particularly in Scotland in the later nineteenth century (as we have already seen, the Scottish student bodies of that time were more like their modern equivalents in seriousness and lack of means than the English student bodies were); indeed something like a federation of student unions in the four Scottish universities was actually brought into being.

Some elements in the English universities tried to copy this, but it was not until after the first world war that the National Union of Students first emerged. It was then more of a device for other purposes than an entity in its own right. Wars generate on their conclusion an impulse towards international co-operation on a variety of levels, and university students were swept up in this trend. An international student movement grew up on the Continent, and in Britain the NUS was formed to provide a mechanism through which British students could take part in it. Inevitably this new grouping devoted a part of its time to domestic questions, but that was not originally a serious part of its work. It was not until the second half of the twentieth century that the climate began to favour its full budding and blossoming.

The chief obstacle was lack of funds. The creation of a voluntary organisation on a national scale is bound to be an expensive business.

Well-to-do students were not interested and the enthusiasts usually had very little money of their own. Finding himself with some spare cash, the average student would probably prefer to spend it on himself. It was to meet this difficulty that the state stepped in to make union membership compulsory, at the same time including the union subscription as part of the local authority grant to each student. In other words, the state now pays for most of the cost of each university student union, the small balance being met by those parents whose incomes are too large for a full grant to be claimed by their children. The details vary, but the general effect is the same. Since the individual subscription is rarely less than £10 per annum and more often £15, university unions are by no means short of money and, provided they supply the basic amenities, few restrictions are made on their use of it. They can affiliate or not to the NUS as they choose, but very few fail to do so. The backsliders are normally those which disaffiliate occasionally for brief intervals by way of protest against the failure of the NUS to be sufficiently left-wing for their taste.

There is much to be said both for and against this system. Social life is an essential part of university life, and in the absence of any collegiate form of organisation it can only be supplied through an active and competent student union. The union manages all Junior Common Room provision, as well as offering facilities for sporting, cultural and political societies. All these are necessary elements in any university, and it is difficult to see how they could be provided in any other way in such monolithic institutions as, say, Sussex, Essex, Leeds, Sheffield, East Anglia, Manchester, Aston and very many more. Students have been conditioned into believing that a university education is a right which they are entitled to enjoy at other people's expense, and it does not occur to them that they should pay for the fringe benefits out of their own pockets. If the public subsidies were withdrawn, the unions would in all probability collapse and their necessary contribution to the quality of university life be destroyed. There is, therefore, a good case, assuming that the present system of free university education is to be maintained, for running the student unions on government money.

On the other hand, it is incontestable that student organisation in Scotland had reached a considerable degree of sophistication before the turn of the century, even though the unions were the voluntary creations of students who were much less well off even than the students of today. They wanted organisation, and they created it on their own initiative. Sir Eric Ashby and Dr Mary Anderson emphasise the quality of these organisations. When eventually a Federation of Scottish Student Unions was established, it too was financed out of the students' own resources.

The NUS, in contrast, owes if not its existence then its continued viability entirely to state subvention. The money is guaranteed and is dependent on no form of student initiative.

This state of affairs has brought certain unfortunate consequences in its train. Primarily, as in the case of the AUT, it has meant the creation of the kind of well-financed power vacuum that is very attractive to the would-be politician. From one point of view there is nothing seriously wrong with this. If one looks at the top, most of the presidents of the NUS have been responsible young people. The presidency is a post that can only be held by those who enjoy uncommonly good political sense. That the NUS tends to the left-wing is irrelevant; students are, on the whole, progressives, and one would expect their organisations to reflect the fact, however unpractical their idealism may be. But when one looks lower down the scale, the situation becomes less attractive. At university level one finds disturbing similarities to events in the lower echelons of the trade union movement. Since the NUS is modelled on the trade unions this is not really surprising. It is in universities that the real power vacuum is found, for although all the students are members of the union the fact that, unlike trade unionists, they neither have to pay their own subscriptions nor find their own means of subsistence, robs them of any incentive to take part in branch meetings and make sure that their money is being well spent. Attendance at branch trade union meetings is poor enough, but at student union meetings it is worse. The student unions, with all their state-given financial resources, are all too prone to finding themselves at the mercy of a small group of activists who are by definition the least interested in the academic welfare of the institutions of which they are members; they are, moreover, able, because of the apathy of the majority of students, to divert funds to their own purposes, not through dishonesty but in the genuine belief that they have a democratic right to do so. There are, of course, natural limits imposed on them; they have to run the JCR facilities well or they would be faced with a mammoth revolt—the bread and circuses rule is one that every politician has to learn—but this leaves them with adequate spare funds. They can be harsh on minorities because they are too small to disturb their hold on power; there is little to stop them from diverting funds to aims that have nothing to do with the university. In short, they are ideally placed to illustrate the famous dictum about the ability of power to corrupt. Lord Acton could not have dreamed up a better laboratory specimen than is offered by many student unions today, for instance the provision of a base for pickets offered by the Essex students' union during the miners' strike, or the not uncommon refusal of facilities to political opponents.

All this amounts to a withdrawal of freedom of choice from the individual student in favour of a no-option package deal. The student gets what the governing clique of the union cares to provide, and becomes whether he likes it or not a supporter of whatever the clique wishes to support. There is a good case, given the current welfare state attitudes, for state provision of JCR facilities in this way. They have to be provided, and it is right that the students themselves should organise them, so a compulsory *per capita* levy can easily be justified. But it is difficult to see a sound reason for non-JCR functions being treated in the same way. Why should a student support a chess club, a tennis club, a negotiating committee with the university authorities or a debating society if his inclinations do not run in these directions? If the total union subscription paid on his behalf is, say, £15 and the actual cost of running the JCR properly is £10, why should he not be allowed to disburse the remaining £5 as he wishes, on sporting clubs, on the dramatic society and on a political club of his own choice? The cost of negotiating with the authorities cannot be great, and it could be left to the interested student to register for a vote in the selection of the negotiating committee for a very small sum. Or, if he wants to spend his £5 on books, or on wine, women and song, why not? That is the way one learns responsibility, which it is a prime function of a university to teach. The collectivists have not helped university aims by insisting on a package deal. All that they have achieved is an excess of politics in the university atmosphere, as much to the detriment of those who take advantage of it as it to is those who stand aloof.

To round off this chapter, let us take a look at the Bolderdale students. In 1972 there were 5,383 of them, 4,755 full-time and 628 part-time. Of the full-time students 2,922 were men and 1,833 women. Nearly all were school-leavers, except for 97 mature students and 587 graduate students. Divided on a class basis, as far as the statistics are available about 1,080 came from working class homes, of whom 553 were part-time students. Less than a dozen women students had working class origins. Unlike many other universities in England, Bolderdale has a high proportion of local students. The three Bolderdale counties have an intense local patriotism, and there is a tradition of local university applicants making it their first choice on their UCCA forms. There is also a tendency on the part of the university to give them preference, although it is under heavy pressure from elsewhere, especially in disciplines such as physics where it is pre-eminent. In 1972, 1,687 men students and 1,192 women students came from the Bolderdale counties. The homes of the remaining 2,504 students were scattered fairly evenly through the rest of the country, except for 318 students from overseas.

Recent vice-chancellors have paid particular attention to student social facilities. The union building is by no means luxurious, but there is plenty of it. It includes a huge lounge and coffee bar, a small leisure library (stocked and operated by the union), two television rooms, a quiet room and a (not so quiet) bar. There is also a refectory, which is used from time to time for dances, and in times of turbulence for meetings. In the Community Centre at University Village there is some lesser accommodation which is not exclusive to students but is shared with them by dons and other university employees. For society meetings, lecture rooms and seminar rooms can be hired at a very moderate charge.

As in most universities, membership of the union is compulsory, and the annual subscription is £15. Discounting a small number of drop-outs, it can therefore be assumed that the annual income of the union is £15 × 5,383, which makes a very substantial figure of just over £80,000. This sum is administered by the union committee with the help of a paid professional staff. The committee is elected by the whole body of students, and there have been occasions when as many as 48% of them have registered their votes. More usually the proportion is around 15%. The rules of the union were carefully thought out, but like all constitutional documents they are totally unknown to the great majority of the people they affect. The number of students who have read, let alone understood, the union rules is miniscule. Of those who do vote in the committee elections, only a small proportion are fully aware of the importance of what they are doing; they vote because voting is a positive act, and people like to perform positive acts.

The ability actually to exercise the authority latent in the union constitution goes to those who have the inclination and ability to master its mechanism. In numbers, they are very few. They are the élite of an élite. The Bolderdale students' union is known as the Bolderdale Guild of Students and was established by the university's original charter. Subsequent amendments to the charter, and also to the university statutes and the Guild's own rules, most of them dating from the post-war period of expansion, have increased its standing considerably. Whereas originally it had a right to 'make representations' to the University Council, it now appoints one member of the Court, three members of the Council and three members of the Academic Senate. None of these representatives may take part in or vote on questions of academic appointments, but in these matters the old right to make representations remains. It is also entitled to appoint two members of the Vice-Chancellor's Disciplinary Committee.

Up to the 1960s there was little friction between students and dons, but during that decade the prevailing university temper was reflected in

Bolderdale. Here it is sufficient to say that, largely because of the efforts of Professor Prime, the Guild has on the whole shown a considerable sense of responsibility in its governmental role, irrespective of the politics of its ruling group. It is only in more recent years, and then only occasionally, that it has got out of hand. Most of the students lack interest in university government and administration, and treat their university more as an environment to be adjusted to than as an area for creative thought and work.

CHAPTER TEN

Protest in universities

There is nothing new under the sun. When today's students demand a say in the appointment of their teachers they are merely following in the footsteps of their predecessors in Salerno eight centuries ago. Salerno was indeed highly modern in many respects. Not only did the students hire and fire their academic staff, they even employed some women among them. In their students' Rectors the Scottish universities preserve a direct descendant of this emphasis on student rights; it is thus scarcely surprising that the first stirrings of the modern student movement in Britain should have come from the north. Salerno, however, was primarily a medical school, and there seems to be an affinity between medicine and experiment. It is much less of an establishment subject than, say, law or theology, both of which are more concerned with defining or even justifying what already exists than in discovering ways of improving it. Since law and theology became the principal subjects of university study, it is not surprising that as the academic community developed the establishment element in it should have prevailed. One result was to create a certain antithesis between the world of the student and that of his mentor, a certain restraint on the former that ran counter to the natural impulse towards freedom of the young; this in turn led to a tradition of student violence that has not yet run its course, for all the sophistic talk about sit-ins being non-violent.

Student violence was not by any means confined within university walls. Much of it arose out of the clash of interest between town and gown. One finds it difficult not to feel sorry for the townsfolk, for the universities, particularly in mediaeval times, were inclined to be overweening and arrogant, and to assume powers over their neighbours of almost feudal dimensions, while the students seemed to welcome the chance of letting off steam in a brawl. One Tuesday in February 1355, a number of 'clerks' from the University of Oxford visited the Swyndlestock Tavern (later the Mermaid) and called for wine from John de Croydon, the vintner. Not liking what was provided, however, a dispute arose and 'snappish words passed between them'. 'At length, the Vintner giving them stubborn and saucy language, they threw the wine and vessel at his head. The Vintner therefore receding with great passion, and aggravating the abuse to those of his family and neighbourhood, several came in, encouraged him not to put up with abuse and withal told him they would faithfully stand by him.'[1] Before long the Vintner's friends were ringing the bells of St Martin to summon the townsmen to action, while the university's Chancellor ordered St Mary's bell to be rung to mobilise gownland. By the next day the battle was at its height, and the university seems to have got the worst of it. Halls were pillaged and set on fire, books destroyed, scholars wounded and murdered. A popular treatment seems to have been skinning the tonsured crowns of the friars. The King appointed a commission to inquire into the 'slaughter', and a corporate vengeance was duly exacted from the townsfolk, the University's authority being much enhanced thereby.

Beside such affairs, which were not at all uncommon in mediaeval times, the recent trouble at Kent University in the United States might seem very small beer, were it not that we now live under the mistaken impression that we have moved into an age when the rule of law prevails. Violence was the norm in the mediaeval world, but it was organised. I doubt if there is less violence in the world today—indeed there is probably considerably more—but it is highly unorganised and canalised so that it impinges less on normal daily life, or is at the worst confined within the comfortable limits of the television screen. This is the peaceable suburban age of the family car and the family outing when what is happening in Africa, Asia, the Middle East or Latin America, or even Belfast or Londonderry, is as remote and unreal as history itself, so that when violence actually flares up within the context of our own lives we are suddenly shocked and appalled. It might help to bring matters into clearer perspective if we could realise that university violence, expressing itself through techniques that reflect the mores of the day, is as natural, even if as regrettable, as the British climate. It needs to be understood rather than condemned.

There are two viewpoints from which student violence ought to be examined. First, there is its general nature as an endemic part of the university system as it has developed. Second, there is the manner in which it manifests itself, which is usually dependent on the current pressures and customs of the day. The first of these automatically brings us to a consideration of student/teacher relationships, which is the subject of the next chapter, but some examination of it is necessary before we

---

[1] Anthony Wood, *The History and Antiquities of the University of Oxford*, published by John Gutch, Oxford, 1786. Quoted in Rashdall, *The Mediaeval Universities*, Vol. III.

can begin to understand the apparent oddities of so many student attitudes today.

It is important to grasp the fact that universities began as completely free associations of individuals. No one was compelled to go to a university, by either the temporal or the clerical power, or by social or economic pressures. These early groups came together virtually spontaneously, attracted by a mutual desire for knowledge. There was no social cachet to be earned, no money to be made out of it, no one to be flattered or wooed or appeased by it. Such rules as there were sprang out of general consent and were not imposed. Efficiency may have been low but morale was high. It was perhaps the purest form of the search for truth that the world has ever seen. It could not remain like that, of course. The world's slow stain always contrives to adulterate purity wherever it dares show its head. Slowly, but effectively, the universities hardened into established institutions, organised, disciplined (after their fashion), hierarchic. It was not all loss; the process of learning and discovery benefited from the greater order brought into the universities' affairs, and even the inertia that comes with growth was not sufficiently strong to prevent innovation. The old staple of medicine, law and theology was allowed to diversify into new branches of knowledge. The universities became islands of comparative quiet and application in a noisy and disorganised world. They had to organise themselves because it was only their own strength that protected them from the greed of monarch and prelate, and maintained their freedom to study as they pleased. They represented the one thing that authority and establishment have always feared—the open and inquiring mind.

Within the universities there was, therefore, a built-in tradition of protest, but protest of a particular kind. They were constantly resisting the pressures of the world of affairs, seeking to live their lives apart from them. They seemed to be crying, 'Stop the world; I want to get off'; but they were in fact exclaiming, 'Your world is unreal; leave us alone to pursue the search for reality.' That was a highly sophisticated attitude, a rejection of most of the things that are Caesar's in favour of at any rate some of the things that are God's. It led, from one point of view, to the ivory tower myth, the belief that universities, because they rejected the power system within which they manifestly had to live, were not concerned with the real world. That was how they were regarded by outsiders. But from the point of view of the academic community wisdom was more important than power; its proper function was to correct, to advise, to provide those who held in their hands the crude weapons of authority with the sophisticated weapons of knowledge and understanding. Grammarian, logician, theologian, mathematician, natural philosopher, geographer, lawyer, rhetorician, in so far as they were true academics they all sought to assert their independence of the kings and bishops who were eager to control them, and instead to set them an example if not of behaviour at least of purpose. What actually happened, of course, was a series of open clashes between universities and authority —municipal, ecclesiastical, royal—in which the universities by no means always came out triumphant.

These manoeuvres were carried out by the Masters of the universities, not by the students. They concerned general politics only by implication, and were firmly rooted in the demand for academic independence. This was primarily a matter of university government, and for all practical purposes most students had been excluded from that aspect of academic activity long before the Middle Ages had run their course. On the other hand, students had their own subjects for protest, both academic in respect of their own grievances against the Masters and public in regard to the activities of the town and on much rarer occasions to general questions of government. Youth is the age of protest, and youth associated with an institution that is itself in a state of opposition to the pressures of established society finds itself in an encouraging milieu for the exercise of its revolutionary inclinations. But at the same time the health of the academic community, its ability to pursue its proper task, demands that student protest should not be allowed to dominate student behaviour. Student discipline, therefore, has always been a matter of prime concern to those responsible for the university's well-being.

We shall come back to this problem in the next chapter. I have raised it here to underline the essential point that protest is an endemic part of university life. It has been less noticeable here than in other countries over the last two centuries, partly because of the unique character of the British universities, few in number, privately endowed, strongly class-based and existing in a social environment in which law and order was well above average. The picture has been otherwise on the Continent, especially in those countries which have lived under frequent violent changes of regime. Where society is unsettled, universities are particularly unsettled, and student protest is apt to play a significant, and sometimes a determining part in social change. It was, after all, a Serbian student who sparked off the conflagration of 1914.

Student protest should not, therefore, be taken lightly. It is a phenomenon that deserves careful study and analysis. What are its roots? In what circumstances is it most likely to thrive? Can it be controlled, and if so how? These are big questions lying outside the scope of this book, but a study of the growth of protest in British universities over the last hundred years or so is essential to an understanding of its nature and quality today. The story has still to be told in more than broad outline, and it is to be hoped that one day soon some social history don will undertake it; there are, however, important lessons to be learned from what we do know. The first is that in the nineteenth century student protest in Britain was comparatively rare, brief and of no great consequence outside the universities. In so far as it was effective, it was in the Scottish universities. In England and Wales the universities pursued a placid course, disturbed at the most by the theological debates that gave birth to the Oxford Movement. Such ferment as there was in the academic community was in the main purely domestic in character.

In Scotland the students became uppity and began making 'demands', though they couched them in courteous and reasoned terms. In addition to the thin thread of tradition of student rights still evidenced by the appointment of a students' Rector, there was the middle and lower class make-up of the Scottish student body which gave it a more serious and earnest attitude to student affairs. In England, the student bodies were either, in the ancient universities, still dominated by the idea of a class élite or, in the civic universities, so new to their situation that no student mind had emerged.

Protest in Scotland was academic in character, concerning the relations between the students and their teachers. It was conducted in a sober, serious manner, more on the level of a disputation than a riot. It took place over the later years of the nineteenth century, and it was successful; Scottish students won themselves a recognised place in the decision-making apparatus of their universities. English students followed slowly in their wake. In neither case did protest exceed constitutional forms, though the threat of it may have been latent. Most significant, the English mimesis was rooted less in the ancient foundations than in the new civic universities where the students were drawn from a wider social class and tended to have the same strong motivation towards learning that distinguished the Scottish students. The conclusion to be drawn is that where the student body is most intimately concerned with the main purpose of academic life one can expect the students to be more aware of their rights and their power.

The basic difference between the Scottish protest and the protest of today is that the former was primarily concerned with academic matters, whereas today it is mainly centred on what are generally called 'human rights'; it has become political in the sense that it is based more on ideology than on practical need. The Scottish student did not think he had a *right* to be at university; he saw it as a privilege, earned by himself or by his parents, and his concern was to make the most of it. The late twentieth-century student is apt to see his presence at university as a right, earned by the examinations he passed to gain admittance, and consequently he feels entitled to make use of the institution, much as we make use of any other public service—health centre, library or even church—for his own purposes. He is less a participant in the work of learning and discovery than an entrepreneur making personal use of the facilities he finds to hand. In response to this change of attitude, student protest has become more shrill in character, less closely associated with university purposes and consequently more disruptive in its results.

It is also less closely confined to the institution in which it takes place. In nineteenth-century Scotland protest was a spontaneous growth, germinating within each university's walls and only later, as it became successful, spreading out to make contact with other equally spontaneous movements. Communications and the mass media have changed all that. Protest is stimulated and encouraged from outside. Reinforcements are sent from one university to another. Mimesis is stimulated by television coverage and the popular Press. Universities no longer live their own lives. They are becoming part of a 'movement', caught up in the social change from individual to collective effort. One can argue both for and against the change. As in all such arguments, those against it plead the quality of what is being changed and are open to the charge of being die-hards, while those in favour look towards the future but cannot tell what the future will bring. Personally, while I believe that student unrest is at root productive since it is right that the establishment should be challenged and made to look a second time at the relevance of its principles, it seems to me that it is most productive when it grows naturally out of its own local discontents, which it knows and understands intimately, but that it can be positively damaging when it is rooted in generalities remote from personal experience and usually irrelevant to everyday university life. Vietnam, Russian anti-semitism, women's rights, apartheid, Rhodesian independence, Billy Graham, poverty, free trade, the Common Market, all these are things that students should argue about and even have punch-ups about, but none of them concerns students alone, and it is no more sensible that they should cause a disruption of university life than that they should bring a factory or a hospital to a stop, or make a mess of family life.

There are limits to legitimate protest, both in the abstract and in the particular, both in public life and in private life. It is very easy to confuse protest with selfishness and bullying, or with sheer lack of self-control. The Malay who runs amok is protesting; he has lost control of himself in a situation he cannot comprehend beyond its inherent beastliness as he understands it. The same is true of many of the public protesters against events they feel symbolic of a world they do not like. When they sit down in Trafalgar Square or stage a sit-in in their university administration building, they are registering their dissent from the circumstances under which they have to live. Most of such protests are ineffective, and their only result is to make the protesters more unhappy than they were before. To be of any value protest must prove effective, and this is more easily achieved by guile than by display. *Suavitur in modo, fortiter in re.* That was the principle followed by the Scottish students of the nineteenth century, and they made useful advances even if they were never wholly successful. They were not violent; they were argumentative, and their arguments were well based. They challenged dons on their own level, and succeeded in making an impression. They had clear views on what they wanted, took the trouble to understand the opposition case and were at pains to present their own views in the manner best calculated to win them a hearing. They relied on persistence rather than on force. They rejected violence as a method and accepted reason. Where they failed, they learned their lesson and tried again. When they demonstrated, which they did on occasion, it was in an ordered manner designed to bolster argument by a display of numbers, not to force the issue.

Protest in that sense goes on in all universities today, but as its news value is nil outsiders hear no more about it than they hear about the innumerable industrial disputes that are settled every year without resort to strikes. The student feedback is of interest to any good don, not only because it is the best test of his own success or failure as a teacher but also because he knows that learning is a two-way process and that the difficulties of his students can help to throw light on his own problems. Student protest becomes valueless and a nuisance when it is unclear in its aims, or when its aims are irrelevant to the academic purpose or, most of all, illogical and violent in character.

Vague protest is hard to deal with. Complaints that 'we are not being helped to fulfil our personalities' or that 'the syllabus is remote from modern society' are rarely accompanied by clear recommendations for reform. They are evidence of general dissatisfaction rather than of concrete aim, and leave most dons unhappy and baffled.

I once listened to Professor Pontifex Prime's reaction to a document presented by a group of second-year undergraduates. It was lengthy, angry and totally unclear. It ranged from Plato to Mao with derogatory references to President Johnson, Neville Chamberlain and Ian Smith thrown in for good measure. The sum of it was that the academic staff was no less than a collection of fascist beasts gorging themselves on the personalities of their unhappy students. 'It's not really important,' he said unhappily. 'It's written by the son of a conservative MP who is busy emancipating himself from his unfortunate heredity. He's popular and has the gift of the gab, but I doubt if half a dozen of the signatories have even read it right through or that any of them understands it better than I do. But it's a measure of our failure in teaching. They all came round waving their arms and shouting, some of them quite offensively, and there's no doubt they feel ill-used; but the root of it lies outside Bolderdale. Where? In their homes? In the schools? In society? These militants arrive without any clear idea of what they are coming to, full of a mess of undigested tripe shovelled out by trendy schoolmasters and emotional amateur politicians, and when they find they're expected to work instead of playing at being grown up, they don't like it. They're a minority, thank God, but they're a minority we have to try and cope with. This particular trouble is more spontaneous than organised,' he added, 'no question of sit-ins or file-burning. Just a general letting off of steam. I think it started out of a complaint about the rise in book prices which God knows has nothing to do with us. The bookshop manager lectured them about using their book grants to buy books instead of pot or contraceptives, and they took that little bit of logic amiss. I doubt whether he was particularly tactful about it.'

Irrelevant protest is much more common and often disturbing. It relates to national politics, and is usually firmly anchored on the left. It is noticeable that it has grown in volume in proportion to the narrowing of the gap between the British and continental university systems. On the Continent, where the universities have been state-operated for centuries, student political demonstrations are frequent and predictable. Here they are a novelty. The nearest thing to a demo that I can recollect in the 1930s was the 'King and Country' debate at Oxford referred to in Chapter Eight, but in spite of all the publicity it achieved it was a perfectly legal and well-mannered affair, conducted according to the best parliamentary rules. Those who spoke and voted for the motion were expressing a legitimate opinion, if not a very widespread one, and in that sense it was a contribution to opinion-forming in the country as a whole. One cannot make any serious complaint over the conclusions of a first-class debating society, however thoroughly one may disagree with them. I doubt, however, if many of those intellectual rebels saw their action as part of a deliberate, organised attempt to force action on the government. The student body produced no assassins, built no barricades, flung no cobblestones. Glasgow's rectorial elections often produced a measure of egg-throwing and as a student there my father once ended up in a police cell after a political meeting which contained a fair salting of students, but that was essentially a public, not a purely student affair.[1]

The idea of students as a class or a pseudo-corporate body never made much headway in Britain until after the second world war, and it is already beginning to look as though the ebullience of the 1960s is on the wane, one would hope permanently. At the time of writing, student organisations seem to be developing more along trade union lines, interested chiefly in such matters as grants, accommodation and jobs. Given the system under which students are the object of government largesse, this is scarcely surprising; they have a common interest in getting as much for themselves as they can, and a perfectly valid right to exert pressure to get it. Their difficulty is that they have very little real power to put behind their pressure. A student strike would not create a public nuisance—it would not shut down an industry, make it difficult for people to travel, hinder their pleasures or stop them sending letters. It would not even stop the universities, because a 50% effective student strike is the best that could reasonably be expected, and even that is highly improbable; most students are still more interested in their studies than in protest.

In effect, a student strike would be one of the purest forms of non-violence, a kind of hunger strike appealing to the conscience of the nation but putting no more than moral pressure on it. Since moral pressure has rarely been seen to be particularly successful in politics, student organisations are themselves under considerable pressure to multiply their power by resorting to extra-parliamentary means; and because they are, theoretically, democratic bodies, their leaders can only keep their jobs if they are militant.

The demo and the sit-in are not just clubs for beating the authorities, but are also baits to attract the high-spirited student. They are as much a source of power as a means of using it. They provide what might be called the sub-militants with opportunities for letting off steam. Therefore, parallel with their propaganda and formal negotiations for higher grants or more residences, student leaders welcome opportunities for more active operations. A good 'cause', such as confidential files or the steel gates at the LSE, or external matters such as the South African cricket tour or a local right-wing meeting in support, of, say, the Greek dictatorship regime, is manna from the skies.

In general, demos are staged by the left-wing. Right-wing students

---

[1] The fire brigade turned a hose on him, and my grandmother, apprised of the situation by a friend, bustled down to the police station with a dry suit and change of underclothes and roundly abused the officer in charge. She was a grand old lady.

tend to be staid, parliamentary and, except on the extreme right, with little fire in their bellies. Those called 'hearties' in the 1920s and 1930s, who went round debagging intellectuals or wrecking their rooms, were not engaging in demos; they were simply indulging in the normal bullying games always played by those whose assets are brawn rather than brain. They had no politics. In political terms it is the left, not the right, that creates scenes; those who stand against the establishment are more apt to display strong convictions than those who are for it. Slightly to parody Yeats,

> *The right lacks all conviction, but the left*
> *Is filled with passionate intensity.*

The passions of left-wing students take quite a lot of working off, and student organisers find them a rich source of organisational revenue, rather as the American big-city machines found Irish labourers a sure means of support. That is why student disturbances going beyond what is relevant to academic purposes have become both more frequent and more unpleasant in character. The irresponsibles are encouraged. We have already noted that not only student militants but also a number of dons promote and organise these affairs. This is a novelty in Britain, not because of any former lack of intercourse between dons and students but simply because dons have not, until very recently, regarded student politicial behaviour as a matter in any way of concern to themselves. Now, however, quite a number of dons have started to interest themselves in national politics, and it is scarcely surprising that they should find themselves sharing common political aims with some of their students. What is surprising is the length to which some of them are prepared to go to join with the more disruptive student elements in condoning and even encouraging violence. At one end of the scale was a declaration of sympathy signed by a number of dons at the time of the steel gate riots at the LSE in 1967–68. This was unusual, but could be justified on the grounds that it was a domestic, academic matter—the gates were in effect riot gates and their erection was a sign of something seriously amiss in the School's metabolism. Nevertheless, it was an expression of sympathy with violent action, which is not usually to be expected from those who stand in some authority in relation to the student body; and it was also an organised and public expression of sympathy, which was unnecessary in an institution with ample means for internal expressions of opinion. No institution has much to gain from washing its dirty linen in public, least of all a university which has strong motives for keeping external pressures away from its door.

A more unattractive instance was the affair of the confidential files at

Warwick in 1970. On that occasion, students occupied the administrative offices, opened the filing cabinets and claimed to have found evidence of political discrimination in the confidential files of individual students. The result was widespread disturbances in which certain dons appear to have played an active part, culminating in a Penguin miscellany of highly subjective articles written by students and edited by one of the dons concerned. The damage to the University of Warwick was considerable, as was the contempt into which the whole academic community was brought. Although the public memory is notoriously short-lived, sufficient harm was done to the public image of both student and don to cause public questioning of the whole concept of higher education at state expense.

The Garden House Hotel riot in Cambridge towards the end of 1970, of which mention has already been made, had not the slightest academic content. A private dinner in support of the Greek government was being held at the hotel. Support for a dictatorial regime is not something that appeals to most people living in a democracy, but it is a legitimate activity in which people have a perfect right to engage. However, it had the effect of making the left-wing see red, in more senses than one (though they gladly countenance the rigid repressions of the Russian regime), and a band of students descended on the hotel intent on breaking up the gathering. So effectively did they do this that much damage was done to property and several personal injuries inflicted. Subsequently a number of students were tried on criminal charges, and several of them sentenced to long terms of imprisonment, one of them being ordered to be deported after having served his term. The fact that a don was reported to have shouted encouragements through a loud-speaker to the mob (it was no less than a mob) from the balcony of a nearby building provided, I think, the high-watermark of donnish irresponsibility, and it seems to have marked the end of serious student violence, at any rate for the time being.

These three instances, however, are each in its own way symptomatic both of the pitch to which student revolt can attain and of the quite new phenomenon of staff involvement in it. Normally it is the left-wing don who is involved, but in the LSE affair, admittedly the mildest example of this aspect of the problem, there were one or two surprising signatories to the statement of sympathy with the students. Certainly a new breed of left-wing political don seems to be emerging, quite distinct from the old school typified by such giants as G. D. H. Cole, Harold Laski or Joseph Needham. No one could have been more forthright in their beliefs than these, but one gets the impression that they regarded their views as personal to themselves, and would no more have thought of involving their universities in their aims than they would have started building barricades in the street under any conditions less extreme than an incipient collapse of the democratic system.

Their militant successors are younger and less eminent in their profession. Professor George Browne of Bolderdale is the only one I could name who has reached the eminence of a Chair. More usually they are lecturers or assistant lecturers, not so very far removed from the student state; occasionally they are senior lecturers. There is, for instance, Martin Chulse at Bolderdale. He is a biologist and a good teacher, but he is also a devotee of Mao, and his spare-time occupation is the use of his considerable teaching ability to expound Maoism to various student groups. He is a sturdy, dark-jowled man with a mop of unruly, but not overlong, black hair. Academically, he is a specialist and has been out of touch with the humanities since his early teens. He learned his politics in student societies at Essex and the only political philosophy he has read comes from the far left. His beliefs are as sincerely held as they are logically inept. He sees the student body as an instrument of the proletariat, and sees his duty to be to strengthen it for that purpose. He led the Bolderdale contingent to one of the demonstrations against the Springboks, and has been active in promoting minor sit-ins and demonstrations. His devotion to academic truth is beyond question, and though still in his twenties he has published two papers in learned journals which have earned him considerable praise and helped to build the beginnings of a reputation. Outside his laboratory, however, he is a man with a mission and pursues it with a single-minded zeal which makes him at once the despair of Professor Pontifex Prime and a bright star in the firmament of Professor George Browne. There are many like him scattered through the academic community, but he is almost unique in being a natural scientist; most of the others have been thrown up through the social sciences.

Two years ago, for instance, Bolderdale also boasted Dr Martin Calvary, a tall, gangling Senior Lecturer in Sociology with a messiah complex. Outwardly as respectable as Crippin and inwardly as self-centred as La Nève, as inflexible as the Grand Inquisitor and as fiery as John Knox, he made it his special mission to oust Professor Pontifex Prime. 'Oh, we shifted him,' the professor said to me, unconsciously echoing the words of the policeman at the door of the Dublin Parliament when I mistakenly asked for a Member who had lost his seat. Unlike that Irish casualty, who has returned to farming, Dr Calvary is now editing one of the many lesser known publications of the 'new left'. His family would be in dire straits were it not for his private income and his ability to operate on the Stock Exchange he affects to despise.

Most student protest, and most don-involvement therein, is a product of the malaise from which the academic world has been suffering as a result of its rapid post-war expansion. It may well be that they are passing phenomena. Certainly the pace has slackened since the Garden House affair. Students come and go and their turnover is rapid; consequently student fashions are apt to bloom and droop. The involvement of staff, however, has introduced a new dimension. It is among dons that lasting traditions root themselves and grow. It may well be, therefore, that something of a permanent change is taking place in universities. Before trying to evaluate any such change, it would be as well to take a closer look at relations between dons and their students, both as they have evolved and are still evolving, and as they should be in a university of the highest quality.

CHAPTER ELEVEN

Relations between dons and students

'Whatever they may be in the United States or on the continent of Europe, British students are in law and in fact members of the university just as much as teachers or governors or graduates are. They are not employees, nor customers, nor conscripts, nor adopted sons and daughters. . . .' The quotation is from an essay on 'Student–Teacher Relations' in *University Independence: The Main Questions*.[1] The writer is Professor Harry Ferns, Head of the Department of Political Science at the University of Birmingham. Much of what I say in this chapter has its origin in his wise analysis of a relationship that is unique of its kind. It is almost impossible, he points out, to draw an analogy with any other modern relationship. In an earlier age it might have been possible to equate it with that between master and apprentice, but modern industrial society has virtually emptied the idea of apprenticeship of any meaning. Certainly today's undergraduate does not look on himself as an apprentice, with its undertones of strict discipline and subservience.

Nevertheless, the undergraduate attends university in order to acquire certain skills from those who have already acquired them. His success or otherwise is signalised by the quality of his degree at the end of his course, but what he has learned in the subject he has been studying is in the long run of lesser importance than the skill in learning he has acquired. A First in, say, history or law or chemistry means not that he emerges a fully qualified historian, lawyer or chemist but that he has launched himself on a lifetime of learning in the subject of his choice, equipped with the skills needed to achieve ultimate mastery of it. Assuming that the business of a university is learning and discovery, then the partnership can best be visualised as one between those who are already skilled in these arts and those who come for the express purpose of acquiring these skills themselves.

It has always been the essence of the British university system that on matriculation into a university the undergraduate becomes a member of it, that he immediately acquires legal status within it and is invested with

[1] John H. MacCallum Scott (Ed.), Rex Collings, London, 1971.

certain legal rights and corresponding obligations. He becomes a partner; in the slogan shorthand of today he 'participates'. But at the same time, because the institution is made up of those who are already skilled in its purposes and those who have still to acquire these skills, the rights and obligations of the two groups, the manner of participation of each, necessarily differs. The point to hang on to is that the members of both groups are equally parts of an organic whole, equally elements in the institution's metabolism, each in its own way and within the limits imposed by experience and understanding responsible for its well-being and progress. It is within this context that the relationship between them should be examined.

There are certain factors that underlie this relationship. In the first place, numerically students form by far the largest part of a university; they outnumber the other members by over ten to one. Second, they are, to begin with at any rate, the least skilled members of it, and are there to acquire some of the skills that its dons and administrators already enjoy. Third, they are mostly only temporary members, three years or four being the average limit of their stay; even the 15% or so who eventually join the professional ranks of the academic community normally start their professional lives in universities other than those in which they studied. The don, however, is a long-term member of the university, and his stake in its welfare is higher than that of the bird of passage. Superficially one might say that dons and students stand in a contradictory relationship at most essential points while at the same time being mutually indispensible—setting the stage for a love–hate relationship of mammoth proportions. So one might think, at least, were it not that in the great majority of cases individual and institutional relationships between them have normally been reasonably good. It is only recently that this relationship has been the object of a determined, organised and persistent assault. Since its defences are natural and not contrived, organic rather than created for the purpose, a relationship of that kind is just as vulnerable as the human body to any new kind of germ imported from another part of the world.[1]

[1] An interesting sidelight on this vulnerability will be found in *The Times Higher Education Supplement* of 24 March 1972. In a front-page article Dr David Craig, a Senior Lecturer in English at the University of Lancaster, speaks of the students as 'rank and file', a military analogy implying strict discipline under law and a drilled mentality. In an article on a later page of the same issue it is disclosed, with an implied satisfaction on the writer's part, that Dr Craig is a member of the Communist Party. The interest in this lies less in the hierarchic symbolism that, on a Marxian basis, equates students with cannon fodder, than in Dr Craig's straight communist technique of using the vocabulary of the liberal-democratic world to explain his far from liberal-democratic ideas. He talks, for instance, of a 'free university', which means apparently a university without rules,

Taking the analogy of 'the reasonable man', on whom the law sets its sights as the desirable standard of behaviour, one could say that if universities were populated by reasonable dons and reasonable students they would be admirable institutions. Both dons and students, however, seem to be as well equipped with original sin as any other groups: dons because their lives are lived in an atmosphere of authority and superiority which breeds a measure of arrogance in the soul, students because their university experience is usually their first opportunity to sow some wild oats. What is remarkable is that there are so many patient dons and so many earnest students. It speaks volumes for the attraction the academic life exercises on those of balance and goodwill.

Don/student relations should be considered from two main points of view—personal relations between individual dons and individual students, and formal official relations between dons *qua* dons and students *qua* students. It would be fair to say that in the great majority of cases personal relations are still as good as they have ever been. Even the most devoted researcher knows that as a don he has to do some teaching and that it is easier to teach a sympathetic student than a hostile one. Equally, most students are eager to learn and realise that good relations with their teachers are a help rather than a hindrance. But, given that general rule, there are plenty of exceptions. Neither all dons nor all students are friendly by nature. Some are lazy, some overbearing, some shy, some naturally unattractive. There are some universities where personal relationships prove to be particularly difficult, perhaps because of the method of organisation, or because of physical segregation of the teaching staff, or even in one notable case because of a highly self-conscious determination to avoid any form of segregation whatsoever.

The initiative lies with the don where personal relationships are concerned. It is part and parcel of his job. He is the man in possession, the old member; quite apart from his duties as a teacher there are the obligations of hospitality to welcome the newcomer, explain the rules and conventions of the university, set him at his ease and help him to fit in. Even the most shy don can do these things for the shyest of students, and in a well-organised university the average freshman is more likely to be overwhelmed with help than to be overlooked. On the Continent the reverse is all too often true, but in these islands the tradition of hospitality and help is still an integral part of academic life. Where it

---

without examinations, without any authority other than the 'democratic' dictatorship of a student proletariat, a demagogue's dream. Universities offer a fertile field for subversion.

fails to produce an atmosphere of mutual trust the fault is more often than not that of the new arrival. Perhaps he has come with a chip on his shoulder about authority, a more frequent complaint than it was now that schoolchildren are occasionally actively encouraged to organise themselves against their teachers. Perhaps he is a know-all who has arrived feeling superior and rejects all advances because he thinks he has no need of help. Perhaps he is one of the very small minority who look on university life as no more than an opportunity for sex, adventure or showing off. The number of such misfits is small, but they present the conscientious don with a major cross of academic life. There are some dons who make a speciality of dealing with them and notch up their successes as a Red Indian might collect scalps, but the really tough cases are left to find their own feet and settle down after a fashion, or to be sent down if they fail in that.

Most students strike up friendships of a sort with one or more members of the staff, which often extend into later life. Some women students even marry one of their teachers, though the age difference usually inhibits men students from similar arrangements with female tutors. Probably it is a minority of students who get the benefit of a close personal relationship, and there are certainly some who are unlucky in their tutors; but bad personal relations are the exception rather than the rule. At first year level most universities are placid, reasonably happy communities. It is as the student comes out of his shell and the novelty of university life wears off that trouble on the personal level is liable to begin.

This is not to say that all the fault lies on the side of the student. It can lie equally with the don. It is easy and very satisfying to be helpful to a newcomer. It is less easy to deal tactfully with the emerging individual who begins to question or ignore the standards he is expected to observe. This is when the difference between good and bad dons begins to show itself. The don who seemed a 'character' at first may turn out to be arrogant and disdainful, may show favouritism or even a complete loss of interest. Worst of all, he may aim at intellectual domination and refuse to listen to argument instead of patiently accepting and responding to it. Not unnaturally, all dons respond most fully to those students who show the most interest and ability in their studies. That is only human nature—one takes to those who share one's enthusiasms. All the same, interest and ability are different qualities. The don welcomes most those who enjoy both of them; he will often spend an undue portion of his time on those who are interested but not so able. What is most likely to upset him is the able student who lacks interest in his work. We all hate waste, and we hate most of all waste of the things we think most desirable. Waste of an ability to pursue learning and knowledge must strike the don as a pretty young woman entering a convent strikes a man of the world, and he is scarcely to be blamed for resenting it, or for showing his resentment.

The smaller the unit, the easier it is for the student to adjust. Universities where the college system prevails enjoy a great advantage. Instead of suddenly entering on a vast campus, as confusing in its complexity as one of the new macro-departments of modern government, the undergraduate finds himself in a small enclosed community, usually no larger than a medium-sized school, where individuals are quickly identifiable, where he is one of a comparatively small number of newcomers and where his academic welfare is the immediate concern of one of the senior members of the college. He may still be unlucky either in the tutor allotted to him or, indeed, in his own powers of assimilation, but in the latter case especially his chances are better than they would be in a more anonymous foundation like one of the larger civic universities where his staff contacts are hedged round by such defences as 'business hours', by the remoteness of his residence or lodgings from the campus and by the sheer size of it all. In such monolithic surroundings he becomes less of an individual, more of a unit to be processed, and although it can be argued that there is a virtue in having to learn one's way around, that success will produce self-confidence and self-reliance, the casualties are more numerous. A university should offer its best to *all* its members, not just to the select few who are best able to demonstrate the doctrine of survival of the fittest. Dons at monolithic universities are aware of the difficulty, but they also find that their means of dealing with it are correspondingly limited.

It is here that British universities enjoy a major advantage over most of those on the Continent or in America. The tradition is that of the college system, and it lingers on even in those universities most remote in organisation from this ideal. It is to be found in the don/student ratio, which still remains at ten or eleven to one in most institutions; in the efforts made in some of the new universities to approximate to it as closely as physical circumstances and the UGC permit; in experiments such as Bolderdale's University Village; and perhaps most of all in the sense of personal responsibility for students that still infuses all academic staffs. But a pure college system is likely to remain far beyond the finance likely to be available to most universities for as far into the future as one can see. We have moved out of the age of endowment, when universities lived on the benefactions of the past (and the spoils of the Reformation), into the age of deficit financing when the finance officer, the accountant and, above all for so long as the state remains the chief source of finance, the bureaucrat call the tune. The prospects of sound don/student relations are all the dimmer for that.

Institutional relations between dons and students have suffered more than personal relations since 1945. This has been an inevitable consequence of the collectivisation of our social mores, which has produced a 'we and they' attitude in most forms of social organisation. It is an alien concept to the academic community which, as Professor Ferns continually emphasises, is based on unity of purpose. There have always been differences of status and function, but they arise out of individual ability to serve the institution, not out of some arbitrary form of discrimination like sex, religion, age, nationality or class. It is probably the idea of class that has most stimulated the growth of the distinction between staff and student. In its modern context the word 'class' implies membership of a separate and innately hostile group with its own loyalties and obligations. Because one is a don or a student at university, so the argument goes, one automatically assumes obligations towards dons or students at all other universities. This is socio-political nonsense. The loyalties and obligations of both dons and students lie towards learning in general and towards their own institutions in particular, towards truth and the particular organisation within which they pursue it. In the same way those of the journalist lie towards fact and to the newspaper employing him to search for it and report it; those of the stockbroker towards sound investment policy and the clients who employ him. There is a good reason for saying that the fitter or the steelworker or coal miner need to combine to defeat the monopolistic tendencies of their employers; but who, until very recently, ever heard of university administrations combining to repress their dons or students?

Admittedly, some colour may have been given to this idea by the fact that today the state has become the paymaster of both don and student and therefore subjects them to monopolistic conditions. Government is exercising, through the UGC and local authorities, an increasing control over the circumstances under which both dons and students live. It is not surprising, therefore, that each group should take measures to protect itself. In doing so they unfortunately differentiate themselves. Each, once united in effort, learns to have aims antagonistic to the other; the student learns to see himself as subject to the don, the don begins to see himself as a different type of animal from the student. Good relations between groups are never easily come by. It is as if the white and red blood corpuscles in the body organised themselves into separate groups, each aiming at the largest share of the nourishment available. Their job is to complement each other, which they do individually. Collectivise them and they would immediately be at odds. The analogy could be extended. Suppose that the group organisation of corpuscles was infectious, so that it could spread from one person to another. Unchecked this would lead to an epidemic. That is not unlike what the NUS and the AUT are doing to the universities.

The analogy breaks down, however, because the NUS is militant, whereas, as we have seen, the AUT is largely disregarded by the majority of dons when it comes to its political activities. All the same, the mere existence of the two organisations helps to highlight the differences between them and to make good relations more difficult. Apologists for them would of course deny this, but one has only to see how even the best of dons begins to see red when faced by organised student indiscipline to understand how great the damage really is. The don who is really devoted to his students, who will go to endless trouble to help them and to understand their problems, finds himself up against a planned wave of hostility. It is not only that student disturbances disrupt timetables, make study more difficult, wreck seminar arrangements and upset the whole system of administration, but, more insidiously, by emphasising the 'we and they' element they help to destroy the basis of mutual confidence on which teaching and learning are based.

Add to that the behaviour of bad dons who make use of student discontent for their own purposes, and it is not surprising that from time to time relations fast begin to deteriorate, as much within the Senior Common Rooms as between tutor and student. There has always been some measure of strained relations between don and don—it is a part of donnishness—but it has rarely been of a kind to affect a don's relations with his students, however intolerable the protagonists may have made life for each other.

And yet, and yet . . . Professor Pontifex Prime will tell you that there is much to be said for the student militant. More often than not it is he who has the brains, who is the able learner, the most worth taking trouble over. Many employers, personnel managers of staid blue chip firms, will say the same thing. The militants are often intellectually able and have a gift for leadership, and they are hard workers once their interest has been caught. 'No, I don't try to tame them,' Professor Prime corrected me. 'They're not tameable at that age, and its true enough that they never are, some of them. But it could be said, perhaps, that I do house-train one or two here and there. I'm in a fortunate position. Politics is their interest and it's my subject, and that gives me an edge on them. It's an easy subject to make interesting—there's something of the politician in all of us—and the militant's half way in my lap before he's set eyes on me. Good heavens, no, I don't waste time trying to argue with them. There's more time wasted in trying to argue people out of their political convictions than in talking to Catholic converts about the evils of popery. But I do talk to them about political techniques, which is what militancy is about, and it's quite surprising how apt they are to respond. I take a certain amount of pride in the fact that our Bolderdale students are politically more effective than those of other universities, and create less havoc in the process. Yes, I know that many of the militants are sociology students, but I run a second year politics/sociology seminar and a lot of them seem to come to it. My colleague George Browne (you've met him I expect—an able but slightly limited man) disapproves of it. I'm told that on occasions he calls me a sheep stealer—an odd expression for such a loudly-expressed democrat, since I am sure he does not use the term in its theological sense—and I have ventured occasionally to refer to it, in a different context of course, during my seminar. My militants seem somehow to recognise it and to be amused. It is really a little surprising that dear George should be so hostile to my small activities. As I told you, I don't attempt to argue with them about the political views he has instilled into them. I listen and learn. One does not have to study politics deeply to learn that political beliefs are no more than political prejudices, and therefore unarguable. I simply teach technique, and it is wonderful how the discipline of technique mellows conviction. Even the wildest student can be persuaded that it is impossible to make water run uphill, or make the hotter draw additional heat from its cooler neighbour. You'd be surprised how mellow some of our militants become without losing an iota of their genuine detestation of Sir Alec Douglas-Home, or Ian Smith or the Greek colonels, or of their admiration for Che Guevara, Fidel or the IRA. They try their teeth now and then of course. The memory of that wrangle over the sociology lecturer some years ago still rankles with them. The bulk of the students voted the president and committee of the union out of office within a matter of weeks, and of course they were helpless without the union funds at their disposal. It's one of the case studies in my seminar.'

No friend of Pontifex Prime would be surprised over the state of don/student relations at Bolderdale. He is a superb politician in his own right, and a most human man. He knows that the essence of a happy, productive marriage is a flaming row from time to time and the ability of both sides to learn from them. Bolderdale students play a larger part in the organisation of the academic community than in almost any other university outside Scotland, but not in the approved militant manner. Bolderdale militants find themselves on many committees, and Prime sees to it that they are well coached in the tactical arts of committee work—how to make their points with maximum impact, how to accept failure with grace and win sympathy in the future by strategic withdrawal, how to use wit rather than a bludgeon and how to be earnest without being a bore. There are occasional irredeemables, of course, some of whom survive as permanent thorns in the university's flesh. Professor George Browne has a use for them. Happily, they go elsewhere for their higher degrees.

Where Professor Prime confesses himself beaten is in the treatment of the real bad hats, the incorrigibly lazy, the seducers to whom Bolderdale is simply a matter of sex, the drug takers and drug pushers, all types to be found in every university—and every small town for that matter, as in every large factory or office building. Good don/student relations demand their removal, but they too have brains of a sort and use them, and are far from easy to dislodge. They appeal to 'academic freedom', they are active on the left, they know how to make friends and influence people. In a sense, they are active assistants of Professor Prime, for they are apt to overplay their hands and to provide him with the rows from which he periodically emerges with new laurels on his brow. In such cases he can be savage and unforgiving. He is not a deeply religious man, but he does think of God as a kind of Dean of the Human Faculty, and he has an Old Testament gift for wrath. George Browne, who is a Presbyterian, has divined this quality in his rival, and has been known to preach a 'Prime university sermon' at his coffee evenings when particularly exasperated. It is a huge success, for he is a good mimic.

The odd thing is that there is less bad blood between Browne and Prime than either would care to admit. Neither approves of the other's subject. To Browne, academic politics are traditional and sterile. To Prime, sociology is about as valuable a discipline as astrology. But they both believe in quality and recognise it in each other; and they both, each in his own way, believe in good don/student relations. Their rivalry is recognised by the students and both have their student partisans. Prime is the older of the two and draws on more experience. Browne may yet become as beloved a firebrand as Michael Foot.

We have said very little so far about the student's role in maintaining good relations. It should not be overlooked just because the don has a higher responsibility in that field. Even under today's dispensation, when students go to university as a 'right'—or so those who are privileged to gain admission tend to believe (and not a few slip through the admissions procedure on the strength of a galaxy of 'A' levels without having any true bent towards academic work)—the majority are anxious to get the most they can out of it and to win themselves a good degree. They mock their teachers, as it is only natural for the younger to mock the older, but there is an affection in their mocking. They are quick to distinguish the phoney from the sincere.

At Bolderdale Dr Phlogiston has very few friends among them. Mr Helpmate is just a good joke, and a source of pornographic tales which go regular rounds among the freshmen but which an innate sense of good taste on the part of its successive editors has so far kept out of the student magazine, still curiously named *Bolderman* in spite of the efforts of some women student militants to impose something less one-sidedly male. Even Mr Helpmate, however, has his secret partisans among the more romantically inclined. The prosey don, the over-eccentric don, the lazy don, the conceited don all have their student detractors, but relations remain equable as long as they do not impose their failings as a matter of discipline. Students do have rights, and these rights are paramount within the academic community.

Students may not have a right to attend a particular university, or any university for that matter, but once they have been accepted and have matriculated they both acquire rights and are burdened with duties. These are defined partly by the statutes and regulations of the institution and partly by its unwritten traditions. The rights must be granted and the duties observed if the academic community is to thrive. Much of the failure of universities has been due to this elementary fact not being explained clearly to students in advance. They arrive as newly-fledged adults without having a clear idea of what their new state involves, either in general or in relation to their particular university. It should be the job of their tutors to make sure that they understand all the implications, and it is a fair deduction that where serious disturbances have taken place the teaching body has been negligent in that side of its work; for students are no more ill-disposed or malicious in one university than in another, or more than any other group of young people. They are perhaps more easily led, but their instincts are sound and, given encouragement, they will follow the better rather than the worse courses. There are mavericks among them, irreconcilables to whom trouble-making is a way of life; they are more likely to be the jackals of the militants than leaders themselves. And there are also professionals, born revolutionaries to whom a university is no more than a battlefield; these latter tend to be graduates who have learned enough to see undergraduate subversion as a satisfactory career. Universities suffer from both types, but this is largely their own fault; they are responsible for their own admissions.

Schools are to some extent responsible for bad don/student relations. They could do more to prepare their pupils for university life. Instead of concentrating almost exclusively on qualifications and giving the impression that high 'A' level grades are all that are needed, they could find time also to teach the art of living in a community. It is here that the public and grammar schools score; whatever else may be said of them, they do both set standards of behaviour and provide examples of the give and take that oils the machinery of living. All too often an undergraduate matriculates with three top 'A' levels and not an idea of how best to employ them; he just has a feeling that it is now up to the university and the state to make something of him. If schools did more to prepare their pupils for getting the best out of university there would be less need for a book like this.

The sources of bad don/student relations can be summed up very briefly. First, inadequate dons—inadequate either because they are lazy or lack understanding of what it is to be young with the world still in front of you, or because they lack loyalty to their vocation. Second, inadequate students who should never have got into university in the first place and are as incapable of making good use of it as they are of contributing to it. Third, bad schoolmasters who are thinking too much of their own academic record. To be fair, we should mitigate the schoolmasters' responsibility by mentioning our bad educational system which itself concentrates too heavily on paper qualifications and not enough on preparation for life. Examinations there must be, but there is more to it than that. My grandfather was a schoolmaster. He wrote his own epitaph: 'For 48 years he served his native city as teacher of Latin and Greek—and a few other things by the way—to the boys of the High School . . .'.

Bad dons and bad students are few in number. If they bulk large in the picture it is because their potential for mischief is high. On both sides good quality predominates, which is why British universities are still the best in the world. Like other British institutions, they are under attack from the strains and stresses of a new society being born, and their community life is the weakest point in their defences. Fortunately they do enjoy advantages, if only they can summon up the strength and the wit to make use of them. They stand to some degree apart from the affluent society and neither their senior nor their junior members are exclusively devoted to the money game; their immediate goal, if not wholly idealistic, is intellectual rather than practical. They enjoy traditions and standards that will not easily be swept away. The dons are their custodians, the students their future. If they fight for their independence today as they have fought for it in the past, and stand firm against social, political and bureaucratic pressures as they stood firm against Church, king and usurper, they will continue to be communities of true learning and will help to guide us through the storms and shoals that can all too easily be foreseen.

CHAPTER TWELVE

'. . . An able and sufficient man'

What emerges most clearly from the last four chapters is the degree to which British universities have recently come to be dominated by the national political situation, as much over their own internal problems as by the external pressures increasingly being heaped on them. No political observer can fail to have noticed how education has come to the fore as an area of party conflict during the last decade, nor avoid the conclusion that throughout the 1970s it is likely to form a major, if not *the* major, party battleground as far as domestic policies are concerned. All education is caught up in this new emphasis—schools, teachers' colleges, colleges of art, all forms of technical training and universities; as are the staples of political argument—nationalisation versus private enterprise, egalitarianism versus elitism—both of which are aspects of the critical issue that will have to be decided before the turn of the century: the collective as opposed to the individual organisation of society. The struggle for the mind of man is reaching a nodal point, and education is the key to it.

It is not the purpose of this final chapter to argue the rights and wrongs of that struggle. Rather is it to look at the courses open to the universities in the situation in which they find themselves. First, however, it must be admitted that there are many people, either directly engaged in education or influencing its development through their political work, who do not accept the antithesis between individualism and collectivism, and who see collectivism as a necessary means of enlarging individual freedom. Many would not even accept that their views are Marxist at root. They sincerely believe that by increasing state control over the whole field of education they are paving the way towards a millenium, and they are blind to any totalitarian danger. The very existence of this earnest and well-meaning body of activists, eager as a matter of principle to hand over to the state the machinery for moulding the thought of its citizens, is itself a major factor in the problem. Goodwill and sincere concern are to be found on both sides.

Universities are at the storm centre of this struggle. No one would argue that state provision for education was not necessary. The question is more one of degree and method than of principle, but it becomes increasingly acute as one moves up the educational scale. As long as most schooling is state-provided, the inherent dangers can in some degree be met by making it as easy as possible for those parents who wish to do so to opt for alternative institutions without having to pay twice, which is what the present system amounts to; and also by ensuring that state-provided schools enjoy a maximum of independence from bureaucratic control and parents a maximum of choice within what can be made available. The same is largely true of secondary education, though there the need for independence and alternatives is even stronger. It is truer still of technical education and teacher training.

At university level, however, the need for independence is paramount. The whole academic community is adult, and the right to study what you want to study and to teach what you want to teach are both, subject to ability, vital to the academic process. The break with school and training is complete. The student is not under instruction, and under only the minimum discipline needed for the domestic good of the community. He needs help and supervision in his work, but it is of a different order from what he received at school. It is up to him to choose wisely among the courses the university offers and to make the most of them. The don, too, is and must be his own master. From the point of view of both don and student academic freedom is fundamental to their purpose, and from that of society as a whole those engaged in pushing out the frontiers of knowledge should be as little interfered with as the processes of industry and commerce. A legal and social framework is essential, but within that framework independence should be the rule.

The difficulties faced by British universities today spring from three main sources—finance, expansion and the dominant social and political customs of the day.

The first of these has gradually been making itself felt over the last fifty years, slowly at first but at helter-skelter speed over the last decade. What has happened can perhaps best be illustrated by the rate of growth of the University Grants Committee. In 1929–30 it had five full-time employees. By 1949–50 the number had risen to 20, by 1959–60 to 30 and by 1969–70 to 107. Over the same forty-year period the salary bill had risen from £4,255 to £308,800.[1] To these bare statistics it is worth adding the impression of many university administrators that the UGC is now badly understaffed, to judge by the time it takes to get things done. This growth reflects the degree to which UGC responsibilities have increased following the state's assumption of some 90% of total university costs, including provision for the nine new state universities built

[1] Hansard, 27 October 1970. Written answer to a private member's question.

since the war. Public money on that scale must obviously be protected against extravagance and misuse, and no taxpayer is likely to complain over the cost of such supervision; but the effect on universities is frightening. We have looked at some of these effects in earlier chapters. Quite apart from the inevitable standardisation and control, the mere fact of isolating university administration from an all but tangential economic responsibility for such frills as can be financed from private sources introduces an element of unreality into their operation.

Dons and students are affected in the same way. No one in a university today labours under a definitive economic sanction. Barring downright mismanagement or bad behaviour, administrators know that their essential capital and recurrent costs will be met out of the public purse; dons know that their scale salaries will be paid from the same source; and students know that, once admitted, their costs will be met until they have sat their final exams. This featherbedding scarcely creates the kind of atmosphere that will encourage the excellence at which every university should aim. Universities are reduced to the level of other nationalised industries which, for all the brave words spoken about making them pay their way, can scarcely be classed as models of economic efficiency or dynamic innovation.

The root of the trouble, however, lies in ideology, not in finance. Given the need for some state subvention, which is admitted on all sides, there are better methods of supplying it which would allow greater independence to the universities and at the same time transform financial provision from a sedative into a goad. We shall take a look at such possibilities later. First, however, it must be said clearly that the principal reason for failure even to experiment with them is the concerted opposition of the political ideologues who are determined to bring mind-training under the control of the party politician and the bureaucrat. However sincere their purpose, this is a totalitarian aim, an attack on the liberal democratic society. That many of its partisans are inspired by a genuine concern for the educational process is irrelevant; successful revolutionaries invariably draw on the support of those whose hearts are stronger than their heads. For upwards of fifty years the trend has been not just towards securing a greater measure of equality of opportunity, which is a basic object of liberal democracy, but equally towards a rigid, doctrinaire and unjustifiable belief in centralisation and control as the only method of achieving it. The partisans of this belief have interpenetrated much of the educational establishment—the educational Press, the educational unions, the educational bureaucracy and the schools, colleges and universities themselves—and have bred in it a strong resistance to any form of independence and innovation that might threaten its influence. It is here that the real problem is to be found, and it is a daunting one.

Nevertheless, such vested interests, however strong, carry within them the seeds of their own destruction (not all of the Marxian dialectic was wrong; it was in his extrapolation of his principles, many of which were sound, that Marx erred). That much is wrong with our education system is becoming increasingly obvious. Violence in schools, the resurgence of illiteracy, the steady shift of teaching from a vocation to a trade, and in universities the growing failure to meet vocational demands, student unrest and academic disquiet, all add up to a compelling body of evidence that the doctrinaire approach of the collectivists is counterproductive. More and more, thoughtful people are seeking a reversal of these trends, and on the popular plane there is a growing sense of anger and disillusionment. No one could deny, for instance, that the public reputation of universities has been tarnished over the last decade almost beyond recognition. The demand for a new approach is beginning to find expression.

What, in practical terms, can be done? To begin with, the economic facts of university provision could be clearly demonstrated. At present they are hidden behind a screen of make-believe and downright misrepresentation. The true figures are available from the official statistics, but they are never presented in their stark immensity. It costs, on average, at least £1,000 to put one student through university for one year, plus the amount paid him in respect of maintenance—say a total of not less than £1,500. The way this is presented to the public, however, shows a total of only about £500, of which a purely notional figure of from £75 to £100 is called 'fees'. Some £1,000 is undeclared cost, the bill for which has to be met by the ratepayer and taxpayer. Very few are aware of the fact that every student, however wealthy his background, is subsidised to that amount out of public funds. Since the bulk of these funds comes from the working classes, who themselves occupy less than a quarter of available university places, the present system is in effect yet another example of the ability of the middle classes to get their privileges subsidised by their poorer neighbours. It would not in itself restore a proper balance, but it would at least make clear what is happening if the student grant were made up to £1,500 so as to embrace the full cost. The facts would then be known and the universities themselves would be not one whit the worse off: their recurrent costs would be met in full. The student would be none the worse off: his costs would still be met and he would be aware of what they really amounted to. Nor would the taxpayer be hurt any more than he already is. It is a mere matter of honest book-keeping.

Nobody suffers from the truth being published, except of course those who stand to gain by its concealment—in this case those who want to impose their own control on universities. The misrepresentation implicit in the present situation effectively transfers power from the universities to the paymaster bureaucracy. If full costs were paid through the student, the justification for much of the present UGC control could be swept away and the controls implicit in competition could begin to take effect. Certainly the money would still come from state sources, but universities would be responsible to their customers instead of to an anonymous bureaucracy. There is nothing like consumer power for cheapening and improving the end product. As to the danger of waste, it should not be beyond the wit of the UGC to establish precise costings for university education and thus to work out how much each student should be awarded in respect of fees to make his acceptance an economic proposition for the university. Under such a system, universities which ran up a regular deficit through maladministration could, and very properly should, be forced back under UGC control, while those administratively competent to manage their finance well, and lively enough in spirit and innovation to attract students, would enjoy the benefits of independence.

The objection of the educational establishment to this is that such a change would lead to some universities being better than others, to the detriment of those who fail to get in to them. There should be no place for such an attitude in a healthy, virile democracy. Independence and excellence are anathema to the old-fashioned totalitarian socialist. Under a competitive system successful universities might begin to win more support from private sources—foundations, charities, industries—which would make them better still and destroy the drab uniformity the so-called reformers are so anxious to impose. As the drain on the taxpayer lightened, the justification for state interference would diminish. One might even see the emergence of a completely independent university, paid for by students who borrowed their fees against future earnings. It would make mincemeat of those whose inefficiency and lack of enterprise forced them to fall back on state subsidy. Nothing is more revealing of the reactionary quality of the new educational establishment than its attitude towards the proposed Independent University at Buckingham.[1]

[1] This proposal has been some four years in the making, but over that period it has developed from the purest pipe-dream to the status of a fully-fledged project with its opening stages adequately financed. This was achieved through the backing of a number of far-seeing and enlightened benefactors in the face of a scepticism grounded in the difficulty of competing against popular prejudice and the widespread belief that the state can be the fairy godmother of us all. At the time of going to press, the architects are at work on the Buckingham site of

The trendy state educationalists are against it to a man. This is not the place to go into details of the proposal except to say that it is steadily gathering force and is at the time of writing within sight of its objective. What is important in this context is the almost fanatical hostility it has provoked on one side and the goodwill and enthusiasm it has won within the academic world. Another wind of change is blowing, through our universities this time, and the university system will be the ultimate beneficiary.

That, then, is the first step that can be taken: a thorough reorganisation of university finance to loosen the shackles of control.

There are other steps, equally easy to take and likely to be equally refreshing. The channelling of public funds through the individual student instead of through the UGC does not get rid of the disadvantage of withdrawing from the student any responsibility for his own immediate future. It might even intensify the student irresponsibility current in many universities. Here again the remedy is at hand. Britain is one of very few free countries in which the student does not have to contribute to his own costs and upkeep. A one hundred per cent student subsidy is common in the totalitarian countries but rare outside them. Throughout most of western Europe and North America and much of South America students eventually have to repay a part of these costs either to private lending agencies or to the state. The United States has the highest proportion of students to population in the world, and some student contribution is virtually universal there, so it is nonsense to say, as the egalitarians do, that a loan system would exclude deserving candidates. The most deserving candidates are those who want a university education so badly that they are willing to help pay for it. The National Union of Students will naturally rise in wrath against any suggestion of a loan system for Britain, as may the Association of University Teachers and perhaps even the Committee of Vice-Chancellors as well. *Pace* all these upholders of the *status quo*, it is a reform that must eventually come because the public purse is not large enough to support fully all would-be university students for whom provision could be made.

A loan system, when adopted, will be pure gain for both universities and students. It will provide universities with students more clearly motivated towards study and learning and will give the students themselves a more valid right to a say in university life; they will become in

---

the first college, and the first senior appointments are being made. Many of the suggestions put forward in this book have been borrowed from the new institution, which will do the same service as pace-setter and measuring rod in higher education as the private schools do in secondary education.

some measure real instead of purely fictitious paymasters. They will be making a personal investment in the institution to which they belong. Their rights will be earned, not begged. The universities need not fear this; the Scottish universities never suffered from a student pressure that sprang from serious personal concern.

There is no serious impediment to this reform other than the party politician's fear of making additional enemies. Even the most vehement opposition will be unable to get over the brute fact that the public purse cannot be stretched to carry indefinitely the whole cost of higher education, particularly if its expansion is to be continued. Nor will the long-suffering public be willing indefinitely to support the anomaly of money needed for hospitals, pensions, housing, schools and the relief of poverty pouring in a growing stream into the hands of adults who better themselves thereby but are unwilling to make any return for the privilege. Loans, when they come, may be brought in slowly, perhaps covering only the inflationary increase at first; but the principle, once established, will spread, and the universities will be helped as much as the taxpayer. Students will be better balanced and their time at university more profitable to them in consequence. This is one of those reforms that can do no undeserved harm to anyone.

Make the university carry the responsibilities that go with independence and give the student the independence that goes with an increasing responsibility for his own well-being, and some at any rate of the current problems of the academic world will be solved.

A third area of reform is the curriculum. To some extent this will be helped by independence and genuine competition, but there is also the inherent difficulty of the inertia and ossification that are apt to grow in all institutions. Here universities must help themselves. No legislation can create enterprise; it can only establish the conditions that encourage it. To begin with, university organisation is in need of a thorough overhaul. Too many fingers are in too many pies. Committees proliferate. Professor Prose, Head of the English Department at Bolderdale, claims that he attends an average of two committees a day in term-time, weekends included. He is, of course, an enthusiast for committee work and the influence that goes with it, but it is an enthusiasm that deserves no encouragement. Committees can be cut down and, more importantly, their membership kept to a minimum and based on responsibility rather than on some vague democratic idea of representation. Administration is rarely assisted by a surfeit of 'democracy' which only helps meddlers to meddle and trouble-makers to make trouble. We looked at some of its drawbacks in Chapter Eight.

Then there is the student feedback. Close liaison between staff and students is vital, but it is wrong to believe that it can be carried out on a representational basis. What the staff needs is the reaction and ideas, difficulties and worries of individual students, *not* the interpretation of them by an elected representative who is bound to reflect his own personal prejudices. Teaching is a highly individual business and it is up to the individual tutor to make sure that he understands the reactions of each of the students under his care and uses this information in departmental committees. There is a good case for student representation where decisions are taken which affect the whole body of students, but it is important that such representation should be based on academic needs, not on political aims. How this can best be achieved is a matter for each university to decide for itself.

The curriculum is one object the committee structure should be designed to shape. Here the vocational function must be held closely in mind. Universities have fallen badly behind in this, as a majority of employers of graduates have explicitly made plain, latterly by cutting down on graduate employment. In virtually every university the appointments officer is the financial Cinderella. Above all other functionaries he deserves a high allotment of the available cash. His task is not simply to find jobs for his students; he must also research into the real requirements of employers and advise on how these can be translated into academic terms. Employers are only partially interested in specialists; they are as concerned, perhaps more concerned, with mental capacity, breadth of vision, ability to discriminate, skill in absorbing and communicating information, enterprise and judgement. Montaigne wrote that the duty of the university student is 'to adorne and enrich his inward minde, desiring rather to shape and institute an able and sufficient man than a bare learned man.' Every student, and every don, too, should have those words in letters of gold on his study wall

Student participation and university discipline offer another field for necessary reform. It is a problem of how, not of whether. Of course students must participate; otherwise a university would be meaningless. There is, however, a distinction between participation and control: one is organic, the other political. The student voice must be heard and fairly considered, but it cannot be decisive in any but a few matters. The mechanism of making it heard is a problem of nuts and bolts, and there is a wide area for experiment. The weight it should carry is an entirely different matter to which there is only one answer. The student has not the knowledge, experience, wisdom, responsibility or continuing interest that would entitle him to power. It is precisely because he still lacks these qualities that he *is* a student. Within certain strict limits he has a right to decide on matters that closely affect himself—JCR or residential facilities, clubs, games, freedom of speech—but he cannot organise a university library or an efficient university bookshop, he can no longer hire and fire his teachers as the students did in the embryo university of Salerno, he does not have the academic knowledge to shape a curriculum. He is entitled to be heard on these issues, but not to decide them.

Another urgent need in British universities today is the de-politicisation of student unions. This is a matter partly of financial control, partly of constitutional arrangement. It is reasonable that students should control their own amenities; it is absurd that they should be provided with state funds for political action. I know of no other group that enjoys such a privilege and have heard no justification for it. No one should question the right of students to engage in politics. On the contrary, they have long been encouraged to do so as long as, like everybody else, they provide their own means. A good debating society, run on parliamentary lines, should be part of JCR provision everywhere. It is possible that a case might be made out for a small subsidy to political party clubs, perhaps in proportion to their membership, though it would not be easy to prevent its abuse. Beyond these reasonable requirements student activists should have to look to their own resources.

It is highly damaging to the universities that student unions as such should be subsidised political forces, capable of independent political initiatives which masquerade as representative of the student body as a whole but are in fact the work of tight little oligarchies. We have looked at various aspects of the present situation in the previous three chapters, and it is clear that it leads to abuse and puts a premium on extremism and violence, that it penalises serious students—who are in a majority— and that it encourages neglect of academic work on the part of the few who give their time to it. All this can be put an end to by the simple process of financial reform and more efficient methods of ensuring a proper representative character. It is particularly important that a student presence on academic committees should be divorced from union control and organised in other ways. It should be quite easy to devise a system of election through grass-root channels in place of appointment by oligarchies which win control of the union machine.[1]

[1] Professor Prime has persuaded the Guild of Students to try an interesting experiment at Bolderdale. Instead of election under the normal Guild constitution, student candidates for university committees will have to be nominated by ten other students. No one may nominate more than one candidate, which will prevent a small group putting forward candidates *en bloc* and ensure a moderately wide spread of interest. Nomination will be published three weeks before the election, and all students will be entitled to vote. The details of the scheme were worked out at one of the Professor's seminars and submitted to a specially convened Guild meeting at which both he and Professor Browne were invited to speak. It won only a narrow majority from a packed hall, but this sufficed.

Such reforms would put no limit on the political freedom of the student. On the contrary, they would enhance it by guarding it against abuse. It is altogether right and proper that students should be free to engage in political activity. What is utterly wrong is that control over this freedom should be exercised by necessarily small, unrepresentative groups of activists. Student politics, as practised under present conditions, are democratic only on paper; the forms are observed but the base is artificial. The bulk of the student body is uninterested, and, let it he said bluntly, uncomprehending, but all are forced to contribute to the power prizes to be won. Since the franchise was lowered to the age of eighteen the student enjoys precisely the same democratic rights as other citizens. It is indefensible that a minority of student activists should by law be awarded additional rights. Quite apart from the effect on the universities, quite apart from non-activists being put at a disadvantage and being made to pay for activities that are harmful to them, the whole system is the worst possible introduction to genuine democratic practice. It should be put a stop to at once.

This brings me to university discipline. I do not say 'student discipline' because personal standards of behaviour should be observed by don and student alike. Any newspaper reader or television viewer is perfectly well aware that the most prominent aspect of university development over the last decade has been a catastrophic decline of university discipline. It is urgent that this decline should be arrested and reversed, though this will not be easy in present circumstances. It is no longer a purely university matter, but part and parcel of a widespread international malaise that has swept the whole of the free world. The essential spirit of freedom is no longer clearly understood. Since the second world war it has been sapped and undermined by the techniques of subversion, chief of which has been the use of the vocabulary of freedom to confuse and dishearten its supporters. I gave one example in the last chapter.[1] There are plenty more; the use of the word 'democracy' to describe regimes just as bestial as that of nazi Germany; the usurpation of the honourable word 'liberal' by those who reject liberal values at every turn; the demand for 'human rights' that are not rights at all; the identification of 'duties' with authoritarianism whereas they are the basis of the self-discipline on which the practice of democracy depends; the substitution of statistical averages for value judgements; the denigration of religion. The list can go on and on. The resulting confusion, uncertainty and doubt run through the whole of society. One sees them in political parties, governments, churches, the professions, business and industry, in schools, on radio and television, even in the two institutions that have

[1] See page 125, footnote.

the strongest overt vested interests in freedom—the Press and the universities themselves.

It is a moral and social failure that cannot be dealt with empirically, a lichen growth that feeds on itself and is rooted in poisoned soil. All social groupings need to cleanse themselves. Social attitudes and beliefs dominate legislation and administration, and cannot be formed by them; but as long as we retain the framework of liberal democracy and enjoy freedom of speech and freedom of thought the debate can continue and a switch in attitudes be achieved. This book is specifically concerned with the universities: what part can they and should they play in developments over the last decades of the century?

Universities have a special responsibility, which is why they are particularly under attack. As the source of much of the leadership in other walks of life, they can do more than most institutions to mould popular outlooks and beliefs. In its devotion to truth and its scepticism over appearance, in its distrust of form and its determination to seek out reality, the university is best equipped to winnow out the specious from the sound and to bring us within a distant glimpse of the eternal, if not into its harbour. It is in the performance of this task that the importance of academic freedom is to be found, and equally it is the reason why so much concentrated effort is being put into its destruction by those whose vested interests lie in shallowness of mind. If universities cannot put their own houses in order, then neither can western society.

University discipline lies at the root of the problem. Vice-chancellors bear a heavy responsibility here, which is not lightened by the pusillanimity of their politician paymasters. There are, unhappily, signs that they are unsure of themselves. Towards the end of 1971 the DES put forward a tentative and not very far-reaching proposal for student union reform. Feeble as it was, the vice-chancellors turned it down, effectively siding with the NUS against it. Nor do they appear to have put out any counter-proposals for reform, though it is obvious to the least discerning eye that much is needed soon.

The first attempt should be made with dons, though it is far from easy to draw a line between legitimate freedom to teach and deliberate subversion of established authority. There is no reason why each university should not draw up its own code of behaviour, which each senior member should be required to accept. Much scandalous behaviour can easily be identified as such. No self-respecting don should encourage disruptive action aimed at securing a decision by force—and it is the purest sophism to say that sit-ins and strikes are not attempts at coercion. We have already seen that by virtue of his position the don carries a higher responsibility for the maintenance of discipline than the student.

The assumption of such responsibility carries with it the duty to bear it. Deliberate neglect of that duty is evidence of unfitness for the position. It only shows how far university standards have been allowed to deteriorate that it should be necessary to draw attention to principles so obvious and so incontestable. However, the situation being what it is, they should be written into all terms of appointment. No doubt there are elements in the AUT that would object, but I am satisfied that in most universities, if all members of the Association voted, the proposal would be accepted by a very large majority.

How discipline over dons should be exercised should be a matter for each university to decide for itself. It is odious that it should have to be exercised at all, but all university discipline will cease to exist unless each teaching body grasps that nettle. There is one further principle which needs to be asserted. Once a disciplinary decision has been reached in accordance with the agreed rules and regulations, any attempt to use force to have it changed should be countered with severity. There is no excuse for giving way.

Student discipline is a more difficult problem, for there is a diminished responsibility which must be taken into account. This is due partly to inexperience, partly to the natural rowdiness of youth and partly to the heavy pressures put on students by those who should know better. Union reform is one element in the answer. A second is tightened admissions procedures, coupled perhaps with a clearer sense of accountability on the part of headmasters making recommendations. It would be utterly wrong for any form of political test to be applied, but overt acts of unsocial character are as relevant as scholarship achievement. A third is the need to make the university's rules and regulations clearly known to all applicants. These should appear—in simple, comprehensive form—in every university prospectus, and all application forms should include a statement to the effect that they have been read and understood and are accepted. This assurance should be repeated on matriculation. I can see no injustice in such a requirement, nor any assumption of superiority since it would apply equally to members of the teaching body. A university is, like a club, a voluntary association governed by members' rules. No one is forced to join a club, but those who do are given a copy of the rules and are expected to observe them. If they persistently flout the rules they lose their membership—and their entrance fee into the bargain.

The real difficulty is how to deal with the hard cases. It is no use saying that life was much easier when it was a matter of a dozen lashes and bread and water for a month; happily we live in a more promising age from that point of view. Offences must be proved according to the rules of evidence; there must be an opportunity to appeal; those who give judgements must be carefully selected; and when all has been said and done and the offence proved, someone still has to decide on what punishment is to be meted out. The principles of the administration of English law provide a sound guide in these matters, and one of them is the independence of the judiciary. There is a good case for employing outsiders at some of the stages of the university disciplinary process. Justice must be *seen* to be done.

If in these final pages I seem to have made my points too roughly or too bluntly, it is because we are sorely in need of a return to basic principles of behaviour. There is nothing new in cant, but it has rarely been more widespread than it is today. Fuzzy thinking, reluctance to take a firm line, uncertainty over both ends and means—these are all symptoms of a malaise that can only be cured by going back to the simplicities of the moral law as they have been stated and restated by the great thinkers, both sacred and profane, throughout the ages. It is too late to compromise any more.

Earlier in this book I suggested that the university is society's prehensile thumb. Society now seems to be busily engaged in weakening the muscles that manipulate it and in stiffening the joint that makes it usable. We are coming to the point at which a clear choice must be made between a world of controlled automata and a world in which there is still an honourable place for Montaigne's 'able and sufficient man'.

British universities (1972)

University	Founded or chartered	Remarks
A. *Ancient foundations*		
Oxford	Thirteenth century	
Cambridge	Thirteenth century	
St Andrews	1410	
Glasgow	1451	
Aberdeen	1494	
Edinburgh	1583	
B. *Civic universities (19th century)*		
Durham	1832	
London	1836	
Aberystwyth	1872	University of Wales, 1893
Manchester	1880	
Cardiff	1883	University of Wales, 1893
Bangor	1884	University of Wales, 1893
Birmingham	1900	
C. *Civic universities (1901–45)*		
Liverpool	1903	
Leeds	1904	
Sheffield	1905	
Queen's, Belfast	1908	
Bristol	1909	
Swansea	1920	University of Wales
Reading	1926	

University	Founded or chartered	Remarks
D. Post-war universities		
(i) *Former university colleges*		
Nottingham	1948	University College, 1881
Southampton	1952	University College, 1902
Hull	1954	University College, 1927
Exeter	1955	University College, 1922
Leicester	1957	University College, 1918
Newcastle-upon-Tyne	1963	University College, 1870
Dundee	1967	University College, 1881
Lampeter	1969	University College, 1912 University of Wales
(ii) *New Foundations*		
Sussex	1961	
Essex	1961	
Keele	1962	University College, 1949
York	1963	
East Anglia	1964	
Kent	1964	
Lancaster	1964	
Stirling	1964	
Ulster	1965	
Warwick	1965	
(iii) *Former Colleges of Advanced Technology*		
Strathclyde	1964	Founded 1776
Aston, Birmingham	1966	Founded 1895
Bath	1966	Founded 1895
Bradford	1966	Founded 1957
Brunel, London	1966	Founded 1957
City, London	1966	Founded 1891
Heriot-Watt, Edinburgh	1966	Founded 1821
Loughborough	1966	Founded 1952
Surrey	1966	Founded 1895
Salford	1967	Founded 1896
(iv) *Former Royal College of Art*		
Royal College of Art, London	1967	Chartered 1896
(v) *The Open University*	1969	

REPUBLIC of IRELAND

University	Founded or chartered	Remarks	
Trinity College, Dublin	1591		
Cork	1845	National University of Ireland,	1908
Galway	1845	National University of Ireland,	1908
National University of Ireland Dublin	1908		

Index